THE CSIRO

Women's Health & Nutrition Guide

THE CSIRO Women's Health & Nutrition Guide

**Dr Jane Bowen,
Assoc. Prof. Bev Muhlhausler
& Gemma Williams**

MACMILLAN
Pan Macmillan Australia

contents

About the authors

Dr Jane Bowen

Jane is a senior scientist and dietitian at CSIRO. After a PhD exploring how different proteins affect our appetite, her research has focused on 'health on the inside' through eating well. She has written *CSIRO Protein Plus* and *The CSIRO Wellbeing Plan for Kids*, and contributed to *The CSIRO Healthy Heart Program* and *The CSIRO Total Wellbeing Diet*. Jane loves the challenge of communicating science in a way that people understand and can use in their everyday lives. She strives to be a healthy, balanced role model for her children, and will talk about food and recipes with anyone.

Associate Professor Bev Muhlhausler

Bev is the Research Director of the Nutrition and Health Program at CSIRO. Before joining CSIRO, Bev spent 14 years researching how maternal and infant nutrition in a baby's first 1000 days impacts lifelong health and wellbeing. This work has seen her publish over 120 scientific papers, and write 15 book chapters. As a mum to two young children, Bev recognises the challenges of juggling work and family demands. For her, good nutrition must be simple and fun, and being active brings the whole family together.

Gemma Williams

Gemma is a CSIRO research dietitian with more than a decade of experience studying human nutrition and translating nutrition science into community resources, wellbeing programs and digital tools. She has a particular interest in improving women's wellbeing through positive life-long eating and activity habits. Gemma's personal experience of raising three sons, as well as caring for her older parents, has brought a deep understanding of the many pressures women experience and how these impact our health.

Contributors

Dr Jessica Grieger

Jessica has a PhD in nutrition and exercise sciences, and is a research fellow at the Robinson Research Institute, University of Adelaide. Jessica studies the impact of nutrition and metabolic health on fertility, pregnancy and child health. As the mother of three young children, she knows first-hand the importance of a healthy diet and lifestyle before and during pregnancy to support a baby's growth and development, along with adjusting to a new lifestyle as a parent.

Dr Naomi Kakoschke

Naomi is a behavioural research scientist at CSIRO. Her PhD in psychology focused on understanding the cognitive drivers of unhealthy eating behaviours. Her recent work has focused on developing mental training techniques that promote healthier eating behaviours. She is also exploring the effects of different eating patterns on cognition and psychological wellbeing. Naomi is passionate about using her knowledge of health-behaviour change to create her own sustainable healthy habits, including daily walks with her dogs and cooking with her family and friends.

Introduction

For more than two decades, the CSIRO, Australia's National Science Agency, has conducted research into understanding the critical role that food and nutrition plays in our health.

This information has been made available to Australians through a series of bestselling books. These books have focused on weight management as well as specific conditions, such as diabetes and gut health. They have become household names – firmly established as trustworthy, evidence-based resources to support eating well and good health. In this latest book, *The CSIRO Women's Health & Nutrition Guide*, we focus on the specific and unique links between nutrition, lifestyle and women's health.

WHY A BOOK FOR WOMEN?

The most obvious reason has to do with our hormones. We have a finely calibrated hormonal system, which plays a critical role in our physiology but can also present challenges across different stages of life. Good nutrition combined with other healthy lifestyle habits can help to manage some of the common emotional and physical effects of fluctuating hormones, from acne in adolescence to changing body shape in menopause.

For women who are thinking about fertility and pregnancy, nutrition plays a particularly pivotal role. Research is increasingly revealing the powerful links between eating well, fertility, healthy pregnancies and the health of the mother and baby in the short and long term. The decision to try for a baby is often a powerful motivator to form or amplify healthy lifestyle habits.

Our eating and lifestyle habits as we head into middle age and beyond are key to warding off many diseases. This includes conditions that disproportionately affect women, such as osteoporosis, and those that affect both men and women, such as diabetes and heart disease.

Women are also often the 'gatekeepers' of food in many households, particularly those with young children, doing the majority of the planning, shopping and cooking. Finding reliable information tailored to the unique needs of women isn't easy. *The CSIRO Women's Health & Nutrition Guide* provides evidence-based, trustworthy advice on what constitutes healthy eating, along with other lifestyle habits that are important to support good health.

NOURISHMENT VERSUS DIETING

There is no denying that excess body weight is a risk factor for developing chronic diseases. And at some stage of our lives, we may find ourselves in a frustrating cycle of weight gain and weight loss or trying indefinitely to reach an unattainable target. This is often reinforced by external influences – both obvious and subtle – on our perceptions of body image and what is portrayed as normal or healthy.

Focusing on the 'number of kilograms' on a scale can get in the way of seeing the bigger picture. Good health is not just about the end goal of body weight. Being active, eating well, not smoking, and limiting or avoiding alcohol are all extremely important behaviours that maximise health and help to avoid disease. And the foundation of these behaviours is establishing habits that we can stick to without having to think about them too much.

For these reasons, *The CSIRO Women's Health & Nutrition Guide* emphasises forming positive lifestyle habits, rather than restriction of kilojoules (calories). It focuses on how to nourish our bodies and support good health now and into the future. This is achieved by explaining the science, shining a spotlight on what to focus effort on and through hypothetical case studies.

Key to our emphasis on nourishment are the 80 delicious recipes contained here, all of which are:

- quick and easy to prepare
- suitable for the entire family
- nutritionally complete.

EMPHASIS ON SELF-CARE

Women have numerous roles at different life stages. There are many ways we combine paid and unpaid work, such as caring for children, older relatives and others. All too often self-care takes a back seat, yet it is essential.

By investing time and effort in eating well and being active, we put ourselves in the best position for a long and productive life. Looking after ourselves is not only beneficial for our physical health, but it has a positive impact on our mental and emotional wellbeing. It also sets a good example to those around us. And while there are clear benefits to building these healthy lifestyle habits from childhood, the good news is that improving the way we eat and move at any age will have a meaningful impact on our health and wellbeing.

The CSIRO Women's Health & Nutrition Guide is a clear step-by-step guide to help you form healthy habits that are backed by research.

Part One of this book provides the scientific background on how to have a healthy lifestyle at every stage of your life.

Part Two helps you turn plans into actions and provides detailed information on the benefits of the core food groups. It also includes practical tips for organising a kitchen, which are designed to make healthy home cooking achievable.

Part Three is a collection of delicious breakfast, lunch, dinner and dessert recipes that provide a model for what healthy eating looks like.

The CSIRO is committed to providing Australians with the best possible nutrition advice. This book outlines what we can do to benefit our health, and the health of those we love.

PART ONE

a healthy lifestyle

lifestyle

AT EVERY LIFE STAGE

Hormones – a key player in our health and wellbeing

In addition to what we eat, how active we are and our other major lifestyle habits, there is another key determinant of women's health: our hormones. Love them or hate them, they are an integral part of who we are and how we experience life. The profound effect hormones have on our bodies and minds can be a bit confusing and, because of this, they are often misunderstood. So, let's get to know them a bit better.

Hormones are small compounds that circulate in the bloodstream and carry messages to and from organs. Each hormone fits into a specific receptor on a certain organ (like a key into a lock), which means that their actions are very precise. They are essential for our bodies to function normally.

A woman's body undergoes significant and distinct changes over her life, most of which are driven by changes in the levels of sex hormones.

The major female sex hormone is oestrogen, with others including progesterone, follicle stimulating hormone (FSH) and luteinising hormone (LH) also playing important roles.

THE FOUR MAJOR FEMALE SEX HORMONES

OESTROGEN

Supports reproductive and sexual development, which begins when a female reaches puberty

PROGESTERONE

Helps to stabilise the menstrual cycle and prepare the body for pregnancy

FOLLICLE STIMULATING HORMONE (FSH)

Stimulates ovarian follicles (tiny sacs in the ovary that contain immature eggs) to mature during the menstrual cycle

LUTEINISING HORMONE (LH)

Helps control the menstrual cycle and triggers the release of an egg from the ovary (ovulation)

HOW HORMONES CHANGE OVER OUR LIFETIME

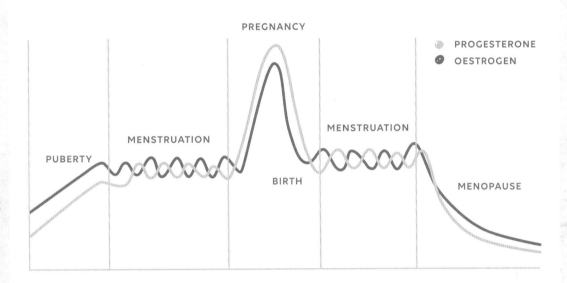

PREGNANCY

● PROGESTERONE
◐ OESTROGEN

MENSTRUATION

PUBERTY

MENSTRUATION

BIRTH

MENOPAUSE

While they are called sex hormones, these hormones influence much more than just the reproductive system, affecting our brain, gut, skin and more. It's not surprising, then, that hormones can make us feel pretty yucky at times – even when they're working the way they should!

While there isn't a magic bullet for managing the symptoms caused by fluctuating hormones, healthy eating habits and staying active can support both psychological and physical health at all life stages. This can help to relieve some of the physical symptoms and manage the effects that our hormones might have on our mood (more on this later).

How hormones change over our lifetime

The level of oestrogen in the female body is very high when we are first born. Levels of oestrogen and progesterone (also high at birth) then decrease over the first few months after birth. These stay low until later in childhood, when they increase dramatically and trigger the first big hormone-driven event – puberty. After puberty, we start having periods (menstruation) and hormone levels rise and fall over the course of each menstrual cycle until menopause, after which levels of both oestrogen and progesterone decrease dramatically. A huge spike in hormone levels occurs during pregnancy; they typically return back to the menstrual cycle pattern soon after birth (as shown in the diagram above).

Puberty

Puberty refers to the physical changes that see us mature from children into adults capable of reproduction.

In females, the start of puberty is triggered by an increase in oestrogen, and this hormone is responsible for most of the physical changes that occur during puberty, including:

- increasing breast size;
- changes in body shape;
- growth of pubic and underarm hair;
- increased growth rate;
- menstruation (periods).

These changes can happen in any order, although menstruation is usually the last. They also tend to come in bursts, rather than in a regular pattern.

On average, puberty starts around the age of 10, but there is a very wide range from 7 to 16 years, and it usually lasts for 3–4 years. It isn't known why some people enter puberty earlier or later than others. Two possible reasons are body size and genetics. People who are taller and/or heavier tend to start puberty earlier, but there isn't a clear link between what we eat and the timing of puberty. Genetics also plays a part, and most of us will start our periods at about the same age that our mother did.

THE MENSTRUAL CYCLE

Menstruation usually starts in the final stage of puberty, around the age of 13 (although again this varies). The main purpose of the menstrual cycle is to prepare the uterus to receive a fertilised egg to start a pregnancy. If a fertilised egg reaches the prepared lining of the uterus, it may attach and embed, and start to develop. For this reason, a missed period is often the first sign that a woman is pregnant. If the egg isn't fertilised by sperm then it doesn't embed in the uterus, and the lining breaks down and is shed, in preparation for a new egg.

The menstrual cycle lasts for 28 days on average, but the regularity of periods varies a lot between women. While the reason for this is not fully understood, it is known that the time between periods can be affected by a range of factors, including stress, changes in eating habits, intense exercise, weight gain and weight loss.

The menstrual cycle is divided into four different phases:

▶ **MENSTRUAL PHASE.** The first stage of the menstrual cycle and when you get your period. This phase starts if no fertilised egg developed in the previous cycle. As the unfertilised egg breaks down, levels of oestrogen and progesterone fall and the lining of the uterus (also called the endometrial lining) starts to break down. The broken-down tissue, along with a small amount of blood, is then passed from the body through the vagina. The amount of blood and tissue, and how long this phase of the cycle lasts, varies both between women and between menstrual cycles in the same woman.

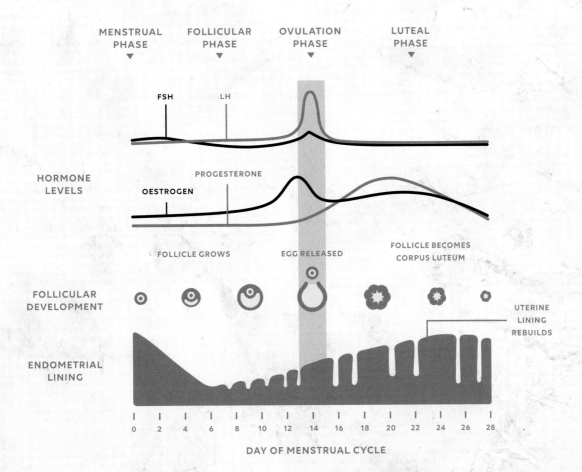

MENSTRUAL PHASE ▼   **FOLLICULAR PHASE** ▼   **OVULATION PHASE** ▼   **LUTEAL PHASE** ▼

FSH   LH

HORMONE LEVELS

PROGESTERONE

OESTROGEN

FOLLICLE GROWS   EGG RELEASED   FOLLICLE BECOMES CORPUS LUTEUM

FOLLICULAR DEVELOPMENT

UTERINE LINING REBUILDS

ENDOMETRIAL LINING

0 2 4 6 8 10 12 14 16 18 20 22 24 26 28

DAY OF MENSTRUAL CYCLE

▶ **FOLLICULAR PHASE.** Follicle stimulating hormone (FSH) causes the ovaries to produce 5–20 tiny sacs (called follicles), each of which contains an immature egg (or ovum). The healthiest of these eggs will start to mature, setting off a surge of oestrogen, and this causes the lining of the uterus to thicken.

▶ **OVULATION PHASE.** When the egg is mature, the pituitary gland produces luteinising hormone (LH). This causes the mature egg to burst out of the follicle and leave the ovary. This is called ovulation and is the time during the menstrual cycle when you can conceive. Ovulation lasts about 24 hours, and after this the egg will die if it has not been fertilised. You can also get pregnant if sexual intercourse takes place before ovulation, because sperm can survive in the fallopian tube for up to 5 days.

▶ **LUTEAL PHASE.** The empty follicle (now called the corpus luteum) starts to produce progesterone, which makes the lining of the uterus ready to accept a fertilised egg. If conception does not occur or an embryo fails to implant, the corpus luteum will shrink, causing hormone levels to fall and the onset of the menstrual phase.

These major changes in hormone levels across the menstrual cycle cause a lot of physical changes in the uterus, and can also cause other effects such as sore or swollen breasts, stomach pain and cramps, and headaches. Not surprisingly, these hormonal fluctuations can also have unwanted effects on the way we feel.

Period pain

Menstrual cramps are very common. They seem to be due to changes in the levels of an inflammatory compound called prostacyclin, causing muscles in the uterus to contract. Adjusting what you eat won't help with this pain, but being active can reduce the discomfort, so try to keep your body moving. You can also use heat (wheat bags or hot water bottles) or over-the-counter pain medication (according to the directions) to make you more comfortable when you're sitting still or trying to sleep. For most women, period pain lasts a few days and can be effectively managed. However, if the cramps are severe or last for longer, talk to your GP.

Emotions

The fluctuations in hormones during the menstrual cycle can lead to mood changes, and it's not unusual to feel more teary or irritable at certain points in your cycle. Mood swings are also not unusual – one minute you're feeling fine, then something that normally wouldn't bother you may leave you feeling angry, irritable or sad. While it's not fully understood exactly why this happens, different hormones have different effects on our brain. Higher levels of oestrogen may make us feel angry and irritable, while higher levels of progesterone sometimes make us feel sad, teary and anxious.

Changes in oestrogen and progesterone levels also influence levels of serotonin. In some women, serotonin levels drop as oestrogen drops in the second half of the menstrual cycle, and low serotonin levels can make you feel sad or depressed. These changes might also lead to food cravings or to trouble sleeping.

Pre-menstrual syndrome (PMS)

Oestrogen and serotonin levels tend to be lowest in the 2 weeks before your period, so this is the time when you may feel the most tired, depressed or flat. For this reason, these changes in mood are often referred to as pre-menstrual syndrome or PMS. However, it's important to remember that hormone levels are continually changing across the cycle, so mood changes can happen at other times as well. Dairy and other calcium-rich foods and wholegrain foods (which are high in B vitamins) have been shown to help some women manage PMS symptoms and improve their mood, along with adequate vitamin D (see page 50). If you haven't been eating these foods for a while, it might take a few cycles before you notice the benefits of boosting your intake and the effect may be subtle. Being active can also improve PMS feelings.

Hormones and acne

The changes in hormone levels during puberty increase oil levels in the skin and cause pores to swell shut, trapping dirt and oil, which can lead to acne. The role of specific foods and food groups in causing or curing acne has been a hot topic for decades. There is now good evidence that avoiding high-glycaemic index (GI) carbohydrate foods (see page 66) can help to reduce skin inflammation and decrease oil production. This means switching to wholegrain breads and cereals and minimising or avoiding foods with added sugar, and sugary drinks.

STAYING WELL THROUGHOUT PUBERTY

Eating well and being active throughout puberty are really important for optimal growth and development. Eating well is especially important during adolescence because this is the time when long-term eating habits are formed. However, many adolescents struggle to eat well, for various reasons. As they explore their independence, making their own food and drink choices can take on more importance. Studies show that these dietary choices are often less healthy, which can make it hard for adolescents to get the right amount of the right nutrients.

Body image concerns are also common as adolescents adjust to significant changes in their body shape. Some teenagers might restrict food intake at a time when they need nutrients more than ever before. The growth spurts that occur during puberty rely on a surge in energy intake. Appetite increases to match the need for higher amounts of energy and nutrients such as protein, iron, calcium, zinc and folate. Protein is important for building muscle, iron supports the expansion of blood volume and helps to overcome the effects of blood loss due to periods, and calcium supports bone growth and development. Zinc and folate are important for growth and development. Not getting enough of these, and other, nutrients during this time can have long-term consequences for muscle growth and bone strength, as well as negative impacts on reproductive health.

Iron requirements are particularly high during puberty. While red meat is the best source of iron, puberty is a time when some adolescents choose to eat less meat. Eating 100–150 g of lean red meat a couple of times a week can go a long way towards achieving iron needs, but other sources of iron are listed on page 69.

If you can't get enough iron from the foods you eat, iron supplements could be needed. The only way to know whether you need an iron supplement is to have your blood levels tested by your GP. Taking iron supplements together with food or drinks that are high in vitamin C (such as orange juice) will increase iron absorption.

Some iron supplements can cause constipation, but many are now designed to minimise this side effect. Constipation is also less likely if you take the supplement with a meal.

Case Study • Caitlyn

Caitlyn had just turned 13. Her skin had started to feel oily and she noticed pimples appearing on her face. She'd heard that you get more pimples during puberty, but this was such bad timing because she'd just started high school! She tried washing her face more often, but it didn't seem to help. It also felt embarrassing to ask her parents for advice.

Caitlyn read that some foods could make acne worse, so she decided to pay more attention to what she was eating and drinking. Now that she was walking home from school in the afternoons, she had started buying sugary snacks and drinks on the way. Caitlyn realised this was something she hadn't done much previously.

She made some changes by bringing a bottle of water with her for the walk, and she also made sure that she took fruit to school, which she could eat as a snack during the day as well as on the way home. After just a few days, Caitlyn started to notice her energy levels were higher and, after a couple of weeks, she found that she was getting fewer pimples.

The changes didn't clear up her acne entirely, but Caitlyn felt so much better about herself. While she found it embarrassing to talk to her parents about what she was going through, she decided it was important to tell them how she was feeling. She explained that while it was great that they trusted her with a bit of money for the walk home, she had learned that growing up also meant that she had to make responsible choices about her lifestyle. It felt really good to be able to open up to her parents.

After this conversation, Caitlyn and her parents talked in more detail about growing up and making healthy lifestyle choices, which really helped the whole family. Caitlyn felt that she had her parents' support to help with all the changes she was going through, and her parents were reminded of the importance of starting these conversations, and hearing what their daughter had to say.

HELPING YOUNG WOMEN THROUGH PUBERTY

Puberty can be a challenging time for both the young woman going through it and her family. The hormonal and physical changes, combined with pressures of peer dynamics and schooling, can affect some young women more than others. For family members, maintaining open communication, respecting personal space and being patient are key, as is encouraging adolescents to stay engaged with family, friends and interests.

Establishing a healthy relationship with food at this stage is a valuable investment for lifelong health. As parents and carers, taking the time to sensitively discuss – using positive language – the reasons for making healthy choices can be helpful.

Here are a few guiding principles:

- Focus on what our bodies can do rather than how they look.
- Avoid commenting on (and comparing) people's weight, size or shape.
- Talk about nourishing the body and the benefits of eating well for growth, sleep and energy.
- Focus on the social and enjoyable aspects of eating and moving our bodies.
- Give some thought to what might be underlying any changes in eating behaviours (bullying, social pressure, anxiety and worry) and encourage open and honest conversations.

We, as women, have enormous influence on how our friends, peers and daughters relate to food and body image. It's important to be mindful of the behaviours and language we use to talk about our bodies and eating. For example, making negative comments about our own (or other people's) body or weight can have a negative impact on ourselves and others. Parents might want to talk about the importance of sensitive language with other family members who might not understand the possible effects of their comments.

Be mindful of your behaviours and the language you use when talking about food and body image.

Early adulthood

There are many lifestyle changes that occur during the transition from adolescence to adulthood. Young women might move out of home (and perhaps back again!), start new and demanding jobs or studies, socialise more, begin long-term relationships, and make more independent food and lifestyle choices.

Some young women start to experience stress that comes with the responsibility of adulthood. In fact, the Australian National Health Survey found that women aged 18–24 years had the highest rate of psychological distress of any age group or sex.

Eating well and staying active have positive effects on our physical and emotional health. Being active can reduce anxiety and stress, improve mood, raise energy levels and help to manage depression. However, we tend to be less active during early adulthood due to less predictable daily routines and many of us dropping out of playing organised sport.

During this period of our lives, our eating habits are less influenced by our family and increasingly by our friends, the people we live and work with, and what we see and hear in the media. There are some positive aspects to this, and many of us use this time to explore new types of foods, expand our cooking repertoire and enjoy social experiences involving cooking and eating with our friends.

However, the messages portrayed in the media, including social media, about what we should and shouldn't be eating can be overwhelming. With the huge volume of information available, it's not always easy to tell which 'eating trends' and nutritional advice are based on proper research. For more on eating trends, see page 25.

While the challenges are many and varied, it's worth the effort of eating and moving well at this stage of life. This time sets the groundwork for a healthy adulthood and reduces the risk of lifestyle diseases such as osteoporosis and diabetes down the track.

Here are some tips that might help as you adjust to a more independent adult lifestyle:

- Learn to cook – it's much cheaper than home delivery. It requires a little bit of planning and organisation, but it is worth it. See page 85 for ideas to 'beat' takeaway.
- Combine exercise with socialising – join a university or social sports team, or organise a 'friends hike' a few times a week.
- Find a healthy routine that you can work into your lifestyle. Invest in a bike and helmet and ride to work or study, combining exercise and zero carbon emissions!
- Review your sleep habits. Making even a few adjustments can promote healthy sleep.
- Check in with your (and your friends') mental health. Are your worries getting the better of you? Take advantage of the online, mobile app and in-person support from Beyond Blue, headspace and Black Dog Institute.

Case Study • Tamala

Tamala had always considered herself to be on top of her game when it came to her health. She never gave up netball, even when study got a bit intense. She ate plenty of fruit and veg – thanks mostly to her mum cooking her evening meals – even if she had to heat it up after training. When she won her dream job and moved out of home, she found herself living a different lifestyle.

Tamala soon noticed she was becoming constipated, which was uncomfortable, and her tummy was making some embarrassing gurgling sounds. When she took a moment to think about her eating habits since moving out of home, she realised preprepared food had started to replace the home-cooked meals. She was in the habit of having a slice of banana bread and a latte from the café near work as a late breakfast and was ordering takeaway for dinner most nights – not many veggies there! It took a few chats with her mum to realise she was eating much less fibre than her body needed.

Tamala wanted to make more effort to 'eat better' but she felt overwhelmed at the thought of it. But by taking it one meal at a time, she gradually made positive changes that she could manage even when time was tight. She started focusing on breakfast by preparing some overnight oats soaked with milk and dried fruit in a jar. While she still couldn't stomach breakfast first thing, she enjoyed eating the oats later at work instead of banana bread. After a few weeks, she started taking a piece of fruit to work and keeping a large bottle of water on her desk to sip on throughout the day. Within a few months, she noticed she was looking forward to her 'desk breakfast' and was ready to make more of an effort with her evening meals. She decided to make a curry or soup containing plenty of vegetables each Sunday so there was something nutritious ready to heat up no matter what time she got home. She still felt tired by the end of the week but that was more to do with work. Her constipation settled and she was actually really enjoying nourishing her body with her own home-cooked food.

FOOD ALLERGIES AND INTOLERANCES

People avoid certain foods or food groups for a range of reasons, including allergies and intolerances, as well as ethical and religious beliefs, not all of which are related to health benefits.

A food allergy involves the immune system. The severity of allergic reactions to a food varies considerably. For some people, they might get an itchy throat, a rash or diarrhoea. For others, consuming just a tiny amount of the food that triggers the allergy can be serious – even life-threatening – so it must be avoided.

On the other hand, a food intolerance or food sensitivity is due to the body having trouble breaking down the food. People with a food intolerance can usually have small amounts of the food without a reaction, but larger quantities can cause unpleasant side effects. This type of food avoidance is often instigated without any formal, medically diagnosed condition. In many cases, this can be a harmless approach. However, if the level of avoidance or restriction is extreme, then there's a risk of missing out on important nutrients – and that can have negative health effects. It is important to note that each of the intolerances listed below should be diagnosed in consultation with an Accredited Practising Dietitian or GP.

DAIRY

Some people need to completely avoid dairy products because of a diagnosed milk allergy, or limit their intake of dairy because of lactose intolerance (a reduced ability to digest a naturally occurring sugar in milk). A growing number of people also choose not to consume dairy products for personal reasons. If you avoid dairy products, replace them with calcium-fortified and unsweetened alternatives (see page 71).

GLUTEN

One per cent of Australians are diagnosed with coeliac disease, an autoimmune disorder in which the gut lining is damaged by the gluten protein found in wheat, rye, oats and barley. In addition, another 10 per cent have a related condition known as non-coeliac gluten sensitivity. There are no reliable tests for diagnosing non-coeliac gluten sensitivity; instead, it is based on gut and skin symptoms provoked by eating gluten-containing foods. The sensitivities may not be due to the gluten, but rather other substances like FODMAPs (see below). Unless you have coeliac disease, or experience non-coeliac gluten sensitivity symptoms, there are no health benefits to eliminating gluten. Also keep in mind that a 'gluten-free' label does not mean that the product is a healthy choice. It might include more sugar and less fibre, and is often more expensive.

FODMAPS

FODMAP is an acronym that describes a variety of different carbohydrates that can be poorly absorbed in the small intestine. It stands for:

F	= Fermentable (broken down in the gut)
O	= Oligosaccharides (fructans and galacto-oligosaccharides)
D	= Disaccharides (lactose)
M	= Monosaccharides (fructose)
A	= And
P	= Polyols (sorbitol, mannitol, xylitol and maltitol).

For some people, the malabsorption of FODMAPs can cause unpleasant symptoms, including excessive flatulence, bloating, pain, constipation and/or diarrhoea, which can mirror irritable bowel syndrome. FODMAPs come from a wide range of foods and it can be challenging to identify the specific type that causes discomfort.

There is evidence to suggest that people who choose vegetarian foods over the long term have a lower risk of some cancers and heart disease.

VEGETARIAN AND VEGAN DIETS

People who choose a vegan approach to eating exclude all foods that come from animals or are made by animals. This includes all meat, dairy products, eggs, honey and gelatine. People who choose a vegetarian approach, or more specifically lacto-ovo vegetarian, exclude all meat products, but include dairy, eggs and honey. Other variations include lacto-vegetarianism, which excludes meat and eggs but includes dairy, and pescatarianism, which includes fish but excludes other meat sources.

The choice to follow a vegetarian or vegan eating pattern can be motivated by religious or ethical beliefs, taste preference or health considerations. The healthiness of vegetarian and vegan diets depends on which foods are regularly consumed – there are plenty of vegetarian and vegan junk foods available! There is evidence to suggest that people who choose vegetarian foods over the long term have a lower risk of some cancers and heart disease. This may be due to the absence of meat, the increased consumption of vegetables, nuts and seeds, or it may even be the fact that these people also generally have healthier lifestyles.

If you choose to eat only vegetarian or vegan foods, it's important to ensure you are not missing out on nutrients. In particular, you should make sure you include:

- a reliable source of vitamin B12, either from fortified foods or via supplements;
- calcium, iron and zinc, either from fortified foods, such as calcium-fortified soy and nut milks, iron-fortified cereals and breads and fortified yeast spreads or dietary supplements;
- omega-3 fats, such as nuts and seeds, and their oils, or consider a supplement.

Case study • Prisha

Prisha became vegetarian six years ago and over that time, she made fairly typical vegetarian food choices, such as tofu, bean burgers, eggs and milk-based smoothies. She recently progressed to vegan foods – many of her friends were doing the same. She thought she was being health conscious so she was perplexed as to why her periods had stopped and her hair seemed thinner.

After discussing the issues with her GP and having a blood test to check her nutrient levels, Prisha discovered her body was lacking iron, zinc, vitamin B12 and vitamin D, as they were absent from many of the foods she was eating. Her low iron levels accounted for the constant fatigue and headaches she had been experiencing. In addition, she wasn't getting enough energy (kilojoules), and she had lost enough weight to cause amenorrhoea, an absence of menstruation.

Prisha was still committed to the vegan approach in her food choices, so she followed her GP's advice and switched to calcium-fortified milk alternatives and added more zinc-rich foods into her meals, such as legumes, tofu, nuts and seeds. She agreed that dietary supplements of iron, zinc and vitamins B12 and D were also needed.

It took a few months but after gaining a small amount of weight, Prisha's periods returned, she was no longer getting headaches and she had much more energy. She felt confident she now had the skills and knowledge to maintain a long-term, balanced vegan eating pattern.

EATING TRENDS

In addition to avoiding foods for ethical or allergy/intolerance reasons, there are various eating trends that are promoted on social media and by celebrities.

It is not surprising that many of us have tried at least one novel way to improve our eating habits – the promised results can seem very tempting! But any approach to eating that is overly restrictive or extreme is unlikely to be sustainable long term, nor is it likely to be nutritionally balanced.

PALEO

While the message to eat fruit and vegetables and choose wholefoods rather than processed options is a positive one, there are entire food groups (dairy, grains and legumes) missing from this way of eating, and as such this approach does not meet the current nutrient recommendations for Australians. For the record, there was not one 'Paleolithic' eating pattern and there is evidence that people during the Paleolithic time frame did eat grains and legumes.

KETOGENIC REGIME

In general, these regimes promote eating a lot of protein and fat (e.g. meat, fish, eggs, cheese, nuts, seeds, butter, oils) and extremely limited carbohydrate. Due to the lack of carbohydrate, the body needs to use its fat stores for energy; this is called ketosis. When in ketosis, the body derives energy from ketones, small molecules created when fat stores are broken down. Because the range of permitted foods is so narrow, it is difficult to stick to long term. Unless well-planned, this approach is likely to result in an inadequate intake of B vitamins, which are needed for energy metabolism. It may also lead to high intakes of processed meats and unhealthy fats, which is not recommended. Some of the short-term effects include fatigue, constipation, bad breath and dizziness. However, there are nutritionally balanced low-carbohydrate options available (such as The CSIRO Low-Carb Diet) which have been shown to help control blood sugar levels, lower cholesterol and support diabetes management.

FASTING

Variations of fasting regimes, involving fasting for a few days a week or for a set number of hours of each day, have become popular in recent times. These approaches can be effective weight-management strategies for some, but they are linked to disordered eating and can be difficult to follow long term.

'CLEAN' EATING AND RAW FOODS

This approach promotes eating more wholefoods and less processed foods. Overall, this can be healthy and encourages the eating of plenty of fruit, vegetables, nuts and seeds. However, there is a risk of it becoming overly restrictive. It is important to note that some foods are not safe to eat uncooked and can pose significant health risks, including raw eggs, fish or meat and unpasteurised dairy.

SUGAR FREE

There is little doubt that Australians consume too much sugar, which is problematic for our health and our teeth. However, it doesn't need to be avoided altogether. Foods that naturally contain sugar, such as fruit and dairy, are also intrinsically nutritious. In contrast, a highly processed and refined product that contains a 'low energy' sweetener, natural or otherwise, might provide little nutritional benefit at all.

Optimising health before pregnancy

Planning to start a family can be an exciting time in life, but it can also bring challenges and concerns. These include worries about becoming pregnant, having a healthy pregnancy and giving birth to a healthy baby. Focusing on your lifestyle before pregnancy can optimise your chances of getting pregnant and the health of you and your baby during and after pregnancy.

While some of the factors that affect pregnancy, such as pre-existing health conditions and genetics, are out of our control, there are many others that can be changed, including:

- recent eating and activity habits;
- body weight and Body Mass Index (BMI);
- lifestyle – alcohol intake and drinking patterns, smoking, stress and sleep quality.

Do fertility supplements work?

There is no evidence that fertility supplements will help you get pregnant. Eating a balanced selection of foods from across the core food groups (see page 62) will support reproductive health. Sometimes specific nutrient supplements may be advised by your healthcare provider. If you're concerned that you may not be getting enough of the right nutrients, speak to your GP about measuring your nutrient levels to work out if supplements are required.

Use the table opposite as a guide. For some of us, this could also mean reducing intake of foods that don't fit within the six core food groups, such as cakes, chocolate, takeaway foods and chips.

EATING TO SUPPORT FERTILITY

It is important to eat well to help prepare your body to carry a baby. It's less important to focus on specific nutrients (with the exception of folic acid). Instead, nourish your body with a variety of healthy foods from across the six core food groups, including wholegrains, fruits, vegetables, dairy, legumes, meat/alternatives and healthy fats and oils. This will go a long way towards providing your body with the nutrients needed for good health and fertility.

HEALTHY FOODS	BENEFIT TO REPRODUCTIVE HEALTH
Oily (fatty) fish, such as salmon, trout and sardines, provide higher amounts of omega-3 fatty acids. Nuts and seeds, canola oil and some legumes also provide omega-3 fatty acids.	Omega-3 fatty acids may improve egg quality and support embryo implantation and menstrual cycle function.
Wholegrain foods (whole-wheat bread, pasta, crackers, cereals), as well as fruits, vegetables, nuts and seeds, provide fibre.	Fibre may be beneficial for the microbiome in our reproductive organs, which may support hormone balance and reduce levels of inflammation.
Fruit, vegetables and legumes provide folate, and fortified breads and cereals provide folic acid.	Folic acid helps to prevent neural tube defects in the fetus and supports fetal development.
Wholegrain foods, meats, fish and poultry, and some fortified breakfast cereals provide a range of micronutrients, such as iron, iodine, zinc and selenium.	Getting enough of these micronutrients is likely to be important for overall reproductive health.

Folic acid: an important nutrient before and during pregnancy

Folic acid is essential to support the development of the baby's nervous system and to prevent neural tube defects. The Australian National Health and Medical Research Council recommends that all women should take a supplement providing 500 µg/day of folic acid when planning for pregnancy and until the end of the first trimester. Folic acid does not affect fertility. You can find additional details on supplements on page 32.

LIFESTYLE CHANGES TO SUPPORT FERTILITY

In addition to eating well, getting adequate sleep, managing stress and avoiding excess caffeine can all support fertility. You should also avoid alcohol, smoking and other drugs when planning a pregnancy.

Exercising when planning a pregnancy is safe. In fact, physical activity can help reduce stress, improve mood, support the pelvic floor muscles and improve heart health. There is no need to change the type or amount of exercise you already do while trying to conceive, unless you have been told by your GP that certain forms or intensity of exercise are not suitable for you.

If you are an elite athlete, such as a marathon runner or professional sports player, or you regularly undertake extremely vigorous activity, you may find it more difficult to conceive, as this amount of exercise can lead to irregular menstrual cycles. Infrequent cycles mean there are fewer viable eggs available, due to lower amounts of oestrogen. It also means that you don't ovulate as often. This is important, since the days leading up to and immediately after ovulation are the only time during the menstrual cycle that you can conceive. Reducing the frequency and intensity of your exercise may help your hormones and menstrual cycles become more regular.

If you don't already do a lot of exercise, this is a great time to get a little more active. Even gentle exercise, such as walking, can provide benefits. Activities such as yoga and Pilates will also benefit your health as they can reduce stress and improve flexibility.

People are having children later in life. While there are good reasons for this, it is important to know that fertility declines with age in both men and women. This doesn't mean that older women can't get pregnant, but it often takes a bit longer. The risk of pregnancy complications, including gestational diabetes and pre-eclampsia, also increases with age. This is not to say that you shouldn't try to become pregnant, but it is even more important to optimise your health.

Does male health matter?

The father's health also plays a very important role in both successfully conceiving and the health of the baby. Eating well, maintaining a healthy weight, being active, and avoiding smoking, drugs and unhealthy alcohol patterns are important for the health of the sperm (measured by sperm count and motility, or how well they move). Healthy sperm can boost the chances of conceiving and having a healthy pregnancy.

BODY WEIGHT AND FERTILITY

Eating well and being active to achieve a healthy body weight can support fertility. Women who are trying to conceive should aim to have a body mass index (BMI) in the healthy range (see page 38). For some people, this may be difficult to achieve. Moving closer to the healthy weight range by aiming for a realistic amount of weight loss or weight gain will have many health benefits.

Having a high BMI can increase the time it takes to conceive, lead to irregular menstrual cycles and reduce the frequency of ovulation and egg quality.

During pregnancy, a higher BMI can increase the risk of gestational diabetes, hypertension/pre-eclampsia and the need for a caesarean section delivery. Women who develop pre-eclampsia or gestational diabetes are at a higher risk of developing cardiovascular disease or type 2 diabetes in later life. Losing even a small amount of weight can greatly improve your chances of conceiving naturally and having a healthy pregnancy and delivery.

On the flip side, having a low BMI can also impact fertility due to less regular menstrual cycles and less frequent ovulation, which means that it's likely to take longer to conceive. Having a very low BMI can increase the chance of delivering preterm, or having a small baby.

There are many credible resources (including this book) that you can use to get information about healthy eating to support fertility and weight management. If you feel you need extra support, then contact an Accredited Practising Dietitian for help, or speak to your GP.

Does being vegan affect fertility?

Choosing a plant-based approach to eating doesn't affect fertility. However, unless specifically fortified, plant-based foods alone (which make up vegan foods entirely) do not provide adequate vitamin B12. Vitamin B12 is an essential nutrient to support nerve development and function, for DNA and red blood cell production and normal brain function. Human bodies cannot make B12. It is only found in animal-derived foods. For people who choose a vegan dietary pattern (especially long term), a daily vitamin B12 supplement (about 2.6 µg/day) may be needed before, during and after your pregnancy to support the healthy development of your baby.

INFERTILITY

No matter how hard some couples try, sometimes getting pregnant is a struggle. The World Health Organization (WHO) defines infertility as the failure to achieve a clinical pregnancy after 12 months or more of regular unprotected sexual intercourse. In Australia, this affects about one in six couples. If you are under 35, planning a pregnancy, and you have not conceived after one year of unprotected sexual intercourse, it is recommended that you see your GP. If you are 35 or older and have not conceived after 6 months, it is recommended that you see your GP. They may refer you to a gynecologist (a doctor who specialises in women's health, with a focus on the female reproductive system).

REPRODUCTIVE HEALTH DISORDERS

Something that can negatively impact a woman's fertility is if she has one (or more) reproductive health disorders. Reproductive health disorders are becoming increasingly prevalent. There are many different types, but the most common include endometriosis, polycystic ovary syndrome (PCOS) and uterine fibroids.

ENDOMETRIOSIS

Endometriosis is a condition affecting 10 per cent of women of reproductive age. It occurs when cells similar to those that line the uterus (the endometrium) grow outside of the uterus. These cells can't leave the body during menstruation the way that those lining the uterus do; this leads to pain and, over time, creates scar tissue. Symptoms of endometriosis include painful periods, pain during or around ovulation, heavy bleeding or irregular bleeding, fatigue and nausea. The causes are currently unknown. It is usually managed with medication, the use of a progestogen-containing intrauterine device and/or surgery to remove any cysts, nodules or adhesions that might have caused damage. Having endometriosis can make it harder to conceive, but it is still possible to get pregnant and have a healthy pregnancy.

POLYCYSTIC OVARY SYNDROME (PCOS)

PCOS is an endocrine disorder that is characterised by multiple cysts on the ovary and affects approximately 10 per cent of reproductive-age women. Many women who have PCOS have a higher BMI and the condition is also associated with both insulin resistance and high levels of inflammation. PCOS can cause ovulation to slow down or stop. In addition to impacting fertility, PCOS is linked to an increased risk of gestational diabetes, type 2 diabetes and cardiovascular disease. The first line of management is lifestyle change, beginning with eating well and being active.

UTERINE FIBROIDS

Uterine fibroids (leiomyomas) are the most common benign tumours of the female reproductive tract. Most women don't have symptoms; however, uterine fibroids can cause heavy, irregular or prolonged periods, or breakthrough bleeding (bleeding that is not during your usual period). If women do get heavy periods because of a fibroid or fibroids then this can cause period pain. The exact cause of fibroids is unknown. Sometimes women who have fibroids also have endometriosis.

If you suspect that you might have one of these conditions or if you are experiencing any of these symptoms, consult your GP.

Case Study • Stacey

Stacey was 38 years old and trying to get pregnant for the first time. A couple of her friends said they conceived straight away. Stacey had also heard that being over 35 meant that it might be harder to get pregnant, and this worried her. Stacey and her partner hadn't been using any contraception for seven months and she felt like she knew her body pretty well. She was confident about when she was ovulating.

Stacey smoked cigarettes, but she figured that was okay because she wasn't actually pregnant yet (she planned to quit then). She and her partner ate takeaway several times a week because they were both working long hours and didn't have time to cook. Stacey also skipped lunch at work a lot.

Stacey decided to see a GP to find out whether she could do anything to increase her chances of conceiving. The GP firstly reassured Stacey that women over 35 can get pregnant and have healthy babies, which was a huge relief. The GP pointed out that smoking cigarettes reduces fertility. Stacey was so keen to conceive that she immediately joined a support group and took steps to quit. It was hard at first, but she was very motivated by the thought of becoming pregnant.

Stacey and the GP also discussed the food she was eating. Too many takeaways and missed lunches meant that Stacey was getting limited fruit and vegetables. The GP thought that she was likely to be missing out on a lot of micronutrients that were important both for fertility and to support a healthy pregnancy. Stacey felt daunted by the prospect of trying to fix everything, but she knew that forming a few healthier habits now would be easier than when a baby arrived.

Stacey started bringing her lunch to work, making sure that it included some vegetables. She and her partner agreed to share the cooking and have takeaway only once a week. She tried to be more organised and prepare meals on the weekend. Within three months, Stacey was pregnant! They continued to eat well; there was no intention of going back to smoking. The extra money was going to be helpful in getting set up for their new baby.

Optimising health during pregnancy

Becoming pregnant and being pregnant is a unique journey for everyone. No body and no pregnancy are the same. You will go through many changes, affecting you physically, emotionally and mentally. However, one thing that is common to all pregnancies is the benefit of living a healthy lifestyle.

WHAT SHOULD I EAT, AND HOW MUCH?

Even though all the baby's nutrients are provided by you, the increase in the amount of food you need to eat is surprisingly small.

No extra energy is needed in the first trimester. The amount of extra energy you need in the second and third trimesters will depend on your weight when you became pregnant, but is only about the equivalent of a bowl of cereal and an extra serve of vegetables for a woman within a healthy weight range. It is important to focus on getting this extra energy from the core food groups – see pages 34–35 for some examples.

The requirements for some nutrients increase during pregnancy, including omega-3 fatty acids, fibre, folate, iodine, iron, zinc and selenium. To meet these requirements, it's again best to focus on choosing foods from the core food groups. These foods provide the energy and nutrients your body needs to nourish you and your baby.

Each of these core food groups provides different nutrients, so choosing a variety every day will help to support your needs throughout pregnancy, especially the increased energy and micronutrient requirements during the second and third trimesters. Consuming food and drinks that are high in added sugar, salt and saturated fat can mean higher amounts of these unhealthy nutrients being transferred to the baby. This is one reason why some babies are born bigger than the average size for their gestational age. Larger birthweight (more than 4 kg) might make delivery more complicated and have health effects for the baby later in life.

Don't forget about water!

The amount of water you need when you are pregnant is a little higher than before pregnancy because of the expanding extracellular fluid, your baby, and the amniotic fluid that surrounds your baby.

Pregnant women need the equivalent of around 9 cups (2.25 litres) of fluid per day, or about 1 cup (250 ml) more than before pregnancy. However, this does not just have to be water; this amount can also include other fluids such as milk, and the liquid in some foods.

ARE NUTRIENT SUPPLEMENTS NEEDED DURING PREGNANCY?

Over the past few years there has been a substantial increase in the number of pregnancy and breastfeeding supplements available. About 80 per cent of pregnant women in Australia report using some sort of supplement.

Women who are eating well, by including plenty of calcium-rich foods, meat or meat alternatives, wholegrains and fresh fruit and vegetables will most likely be meeting their dietary needs without requiring supplements.

Two nutritional supplements are recommended by the Australian National Health and Medical Research Council, folic acid and iodine:

- Folic acid supplements (500µg each day) are recommended for at least one month before and during the first trimester of pregnancy to help prevent neural tube defects. There is no evidence that taking a folic acid supplement after the first trimester provides any additional benefits and it should be discontinued.

- Iodine is needed to make thyroid hormones and is important to support brain development. Women who are pregnant, breastfeeding or considering pregnancy should take an iodine supplement of 150µg each day.

In addition, there are other supplements that may have benefits for some women:

- A vitamin D supplement may be necessary for women who are pregnant during winter or who have little access to sunlight; vitamin D is important to support bone development.

- For women with a low dietary calcium intake, increased consumption of calcium-rich foods or supplements may be beneficial.

- Women who choose a vegetarian or vegan eating pattern are likely to need a vitamin B12 supplement during pregnancy and while breastfeeding.

- Iron needs are much higher during pregnancy so a supplement may be required, especially if you don't eat much or any red meat.

Before starting any supplements, speak to your GP, midwife or obstetrician. Excessive intake of certain nutrients may cause harm to you or your baby. A blood test to measure your nutrient levels will help to make an informed decision about whether supplements are needed.

Some scientific evidence suggests that omega-3 fatty acid supplements may lower the risk of having a premature baby; however, the benefits of routine supplementation are not fully understood and you are only likely to benefit if your omega-3 levels are low. If you don't eat fish or seafood very often (or at all), then you may consider taking an omega-3 supplement. Currently, there is not enough evidence to show whether a probiotic supplement benefits you or your baby. However, there are also no known risks associated with taking a probiotic supplement if you choose.

What about alcohol?

If you're pregnant, breastfeeding or planning to have a baby, the safest option is to not drink alcohol at all. Alcohol passes through the placenta and can lead to miscarriage, stillbirth, premature birth, birth defects and lower birthweight. Exposure to alcohol at any time before birth also places the baby at risk of fetal alcohol spectrum disorders, which can have a significant impact on your child's brain function and behaviour. Alcohol also passes to the baby via breastmilk. The toxins from cigarettes and other recreational drugs also cross the placenta and are harmful to your baby.

Nourishing foods to include each day during pregnancy

Women don't need any extra energy during the first trimester of pregnancy. However, this is a great time to get into the habit of choosing foods mainly from the six core food groups (see page 62). During the second and third trimesters, women need extra nutrients. To meet these needs, include about three extra servings of core foods each day, with one being an extra serve of vegetables. The examples below are a guide for serving sizes.

VEGETABLES, ESPECIALLY GREEN AND ORANGE

½ cup cooked broccoli, spinach, carrots or pumpkin

1 cup green leafy or raw vegetables

½ cup corn

½ small sweet potato

FRUIT, PREFERABLY FRESH

1 medium banana, apple, orange or pear

2 small kiwi fruit, apricots or plums

1 cup diced or canned fruit with no added sugar

LEGUMES, LEAN MEAT, EGGS AND OILY FISH

½ cup canned or
cooked dried beans,
peas or lentils

80 g cooked lean meat
(100 g raw)

2 large eggs

100 g cooked oily fish
fillet (about 115 g raw)
or 1 small can fish

WHOLEGRAIN FOODS

1 slice bread, ½ medium
roll or flatbread

½ cup cooked wholegrain
rice, pasta or noodles

⅔ cup wheat cereal
flakes or muesli

½ cup cooked oats

NUTS AND SEEDS

30 g nuts, seeds, or nut/seed
butters (peanut butter, tahini)

DAIRY AND ALTERNATIVES

1 cup milk

¾ cup yoghurt

2 slices (40 g)
hard cheese

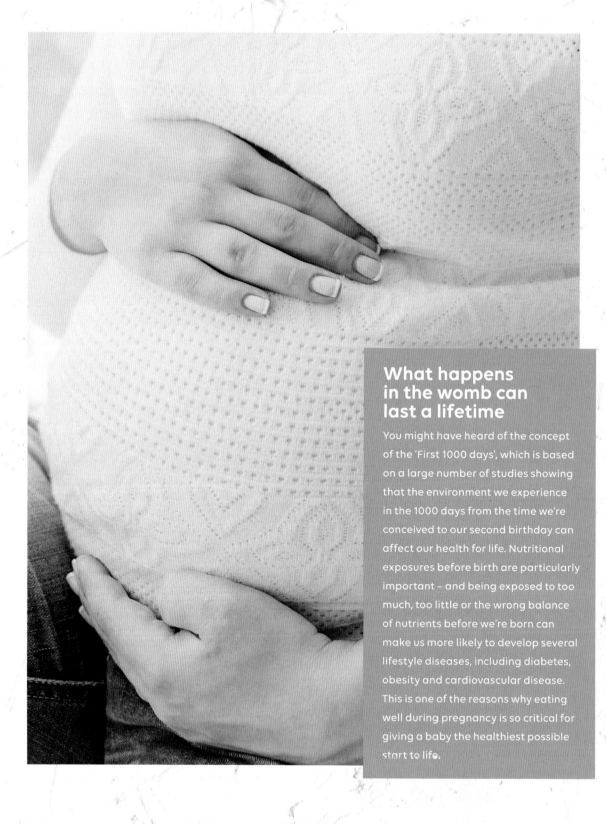

What happens in the womb can last a lifetime

You might have heard of the concept of the 'First 1000 days', which is based on a large number of studies showing that the environment we experience in the 1000 days from the time we're conceived to our second birthday can affect our health for life. Nutritional exposures before birth are particularly important – and being exposed to too much, too little or the wrong balance of nutrients before we're born can make us more likely to develop several lifestyle diseases, including diabetes, obesity and cardiovascular disease. This is one of the reasons why eating well during pregnancy is so critical for giving a baby the healthiest possible start to life.

Pregnancy myths

MYTH

Morning sickness only happens in the morning.

FACT

Morning sickness (feeling nauseous and/or vomiting) during pregnancy can actually occur at any time of day, although it is more common in the morning. This is caused by changes in hormones. It typically improves by about 3 months. Bland foods are often suggested to help reduce symptoms – try plain toast, rice or a banana – and small snacks that are low in fat may also help. Vitamin B6 has also been shown to help reduce symptoms of nausea during pregnancy. Foods rich in B6 include pork, chicken, turkey, peanuts, soy products and oats. If you feel your morning sickness is extreme, talk to your GP, midwife or obstetrician, and check with your doctor before taking any over-the-counter medications or discontinuing supplements during pregnancy. If your morning sickness is severe, you could lose weight. Rest assured, while this time might be difficult for you, your baby will get the nutrients it needs and continue to grow. It's also important to rest when you're not feeling your best. Once your morning sickness has subsided, continue eating well and being active.

MYTH

I can't eat nuts or high allergenic foods while I'm pregnant.

FACT

Research shows that consuming high allergenic foods such as peanuts, dairy and eggs while pregnant does not make your baby become allergic to these foods. In fact, the most recent evidence suggests that eating these foods (assuming that you are not allergic to them yourself!) while you are pregnant and breastfeeding can actually reduce your baby's risk of allergy.

MYTH

I can't consume coffee, tea or any caffeine while I'm pregnant.

FACT

Having small to moderate amounts of caffeine is unlikely to harm you or your baby; that is, no more than 3 small cups of coffee or 6 cups of tea each day (300 mg of caffeine in total). Sugar-sweetened caffeinated beverages, like some soft drinks and energy drinks, should be limited; these drinks are not included in the six food groups. Herbal teas, such as chamomile, ginger and mint, contain no caffeine; green tea contains moderate amounts, but generally less than black tea.

HEALTHY WEIGHT GAIN DURING PREGNANCY

When you're pregnant, your weight will naturally increase because of the growing baby, and more so if you're having twins or triplets. You will also gain weight because of the extra blood volume, the growth of the placenta, fluid, some extra fat storage (which is a normal part of pregnancy) and an increase in breast size.

The recommended range of weight gain for a 'singleton' pregnancy varies depending on a woman's body mass index (BMI) range at the beginning of the pregnancy (see table below).

In the first three months or so, you will not gain much weight – up to 2 kilograms. In the second and third trimesters, there will be a gradual increase. Body shape and weight changes (how and when) are different for everyone, and they won't be even across each week of your pregnancy.

You might be weighed at your antenatal appointments. If you are interested, you may choose to monitor your pregnancy weight gain more often. The table below is an approximate guide to weekly weight gain – remember it is an estimate so expect some variation. Gaining more or less weight than the recommended range can have undesirable consequences for both you and your baby:

- Gaining more than recommended can increase your risk of developing gestational diabetes; your baby may also be born heavier (see page 32).

- If you start your pregnancy underweight and do not gain enough weight during your pregnancy, your baby might be born small or too early (premature). Some research has shown that babies born small may be more at risk of some chronic diseases, including type 2 diabetes, later in life, while babies born too early are more at risk of developmental delay and learning difficulties.

BODY MASS INDEX RANGE BMI calculation = weight (kg) ÷ (height (m) × height (m))	APPROXIMATE WEEKLY WEIGHT GAIN IN THE SECOND AND THIRD TRIMESTERS (SINGLETON PREGNANCY)	TOTAL RECOMMENDED WEIGHT GAIN (SINGLETON PREGNANCY)
UNDER 18.5 (UNDERWEIGHT)	440–580 g	12.5–18 kg
18.5–24.9 (HEALTHY WEIGHT)	350–500 g	11.5–16 kg
25–29.9 (OVERWEIGHT)	230–330 g	7–11.5 kg
30 AND HIGHER (OBESE)	170–270 g	5–9 kg

Table: 2009 Institute of Medicine Washington (DC) guidelines for weight gain and rate of weight gain during pregnancy for women with a singleton pregnancy.

Can I eat fish?

Fish is very nutritious and is the richest food source of omega-3 fats. Fish is also a great source of protein and contains other important vitamins and minerals. Eating cooked fish in pregnancy is safe but consideration needs to be given to the varieties you choose. This is because some may contain higher levels of mercury than others – and therefore carry a risk of mercury poisoning. The good news is most fish contain very low mercury levels, and can safely be eaten 2–3 times a week. These include mackerel, Atlantic salmon, canned salmon and tuna in oil, herrings and sardines. There are only a few types of fish that you should limit while pregnant, including billfish (swordfish/broadbill and marlin), shark/flake, orange roughy and catfish. You should avoid eating more than one serve of these per week.

FOOD SAFETY DURING PREGNANCY

Fortunately, in Australia we have a safe and nutritious food supply with most people generally aware of good food hygiene practices. Despite this, there is still a risk of food poisoning. The effects of food-borne bacteria can be particularly severe in pregnancy, since some can cross the placenta and cause infection in the baby. Because of this, pregnancy is a time when it is especially important to follow good food hygiene practices and take extra care when choosing fresh and preprepared food.

Here are some tips for storing food safely:

- Store food in the fridge below 5°C or in the freezer below 15°C.
- Avoid refreezing thawed foods.
- Store raw food in the fridge separately from (and below) cooked food.
- Thaw food in the fridge, and keep it there until it is ready to be cooked.
- Wait for steaming hot food to cool slightly before putting it in the fridge.
- Reheat food until it is steaming hot.

Listeria

Listeria is a bacteria that is commonly found in water, soil and faeces and can contaminate different types of food. It can cause serious illness and, in rare cases, can cause death. Most people can tolerate small exposures. However, the consequences of listeriosis infection are more severe during pregnancy. Mothers generally experience mild symptoms, but listeriosis can lead to miscarriage, stillbirth or infection of the newborn baby.

To minimise the risk of a listeria infection while pregnant, it is recommended that the following foods are avoided:

- chilled seafood, such as raw oysters, sashimi and sushi, smoked ready-to-eat seafood and cooked ready-to-eat prawns;
- cold meats from delicatessen counters and sandwich bars, and packaged sliced ready-to-eat meat;
- cold cooked ready-to-eat chicken (whole, portions, or diced);
- pâté or meat spreads;
- pre-packaged or premade fruit or vegetable salads;
- soft-serve ice cream;
- unpasteurised dairy products;
- soft, semi-soft and surface-ripened cheeses (pre-packaged and delicatessen) such as brie, camembert, ricotta, feta and blue cheese – soft cheeses in cooked dishes are safe;
- raw mushrooms;
- pre-cut rockmelon.

Safer food choices include home-cooked meats and chicken (including hot takeaway chicken eaten while still steaming hot); preparing your own salads and cooking fresh seafood; hard cheese such as cheddar; and pasteurised dairy products.

Salmonella

Salmonella is a bacteria that can be spread from infected animals to humans through poorly cooked foods such as meats, poultry and eggs. Although less common, it can also be found in milk, raw fruits and vegetables. Salmonella can cause food poisoning, leading to symptoms including nausea, vomiting and diarrhoea and fever. In rare cases, salmonella poisoning can cause miscarriage.

To reduce risk for salmonella poisoning during pregnancy:

- Use separate cutting boards and knives for raw and ready-to-eat food to avoid cross contamination.
- Wash raw fruit and vegetables.
- Cook food thoroughly, especially poultry and eggs, and avoid using eggs with cracked shells or foods containing raw eggs.

Optimising health during breastfeeding

The common phrase 'breast is best' is based on World Health Organization advice that babies should be fed only breastmilk for the first 6 months of their life because of the health advantages for both children and their mums.

Remember that what you eat affects the levels of nutrients in your breastmilk, as well as the taste. This influences the development of your baby's tastebuds and how they accept new tastes when they start solids.

When your baby is around 6 months of age (and not before 4 months), you should start to introduce solid foods. If possible, you should continue to breastfeed your baby while introducing solids. However, there are a variety of reasons why some women cannot or choose not to breastfeed. Every situation is unique, and you should feel empowered to do what is right for you and your family.

If you are breastfeeding, it's important to remember that this is an energy-intensive activity. Even though you will need to increase your energy intake (and are likely to feel hungrier than usual), this isn't a reason to throw healthy eating habits out the window.

See over the page for an indication of how to meet your higher energy needs when breastfeeding. Younger mothers (under 19 years of age) need more energy while they are breastfeeding to support the needs of both themselves and their baby.

Body weight changes after pregnancy

Life with a baby can be pretty hectic. Having a newborn is exhausting and trying to lose weight too soon can make you feel even more tired. If you are breastfeeding, restricting energy and nutrients to lose weight can reduce your breastmilk supply.

However, it is worth noting that this stage of our lives is when your weight can creep up, especially after more than one pregnancy. As described earlier, beginning a pregnancy with a higher BMI can increase the risk of pregnancy complications, so trying to avoid the 'weight creep' during this time is beneficial for your health and for any subsequent pregnancies.

Once you and your baby have 'settled in', try to follow healthy eating habits and be active most days, even if this takes a different form with 'baby on board'.

TAKE ACTION

- ▶ Eat well, including plenty of nutrient-rich foods, to help keep up your energy levels.
- ▶ Keep choosing foods mostly from the six core food groups to meet the increased nutrient needs of breastfeeding.
- ▶ Make sure you are getting enough lean proteins, dairy, nuts and seeds, and legumes.
- ▶ Try to fit in some gentle activity most days.
- ▶ Drink an extra 3–4 cups of water per day.

Additional nourishing foods to include each day when breastfeeding

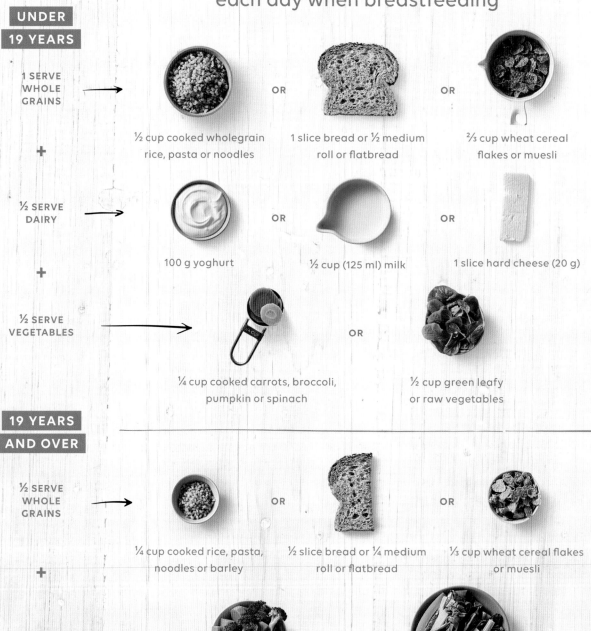

1 SERVE WHOLE GRAINS

½ cup cooked wholegrain rice, pasta or noodles

OR

1 slice bread or ½ medium roll or flatbread

OR

⅔ cup wheat cereal flakes or muesli

+

½ SERVE DAIRY

100 g yoghurt

OR

½ cup (125 ml) milk

OR

1 slice hard cheese (20 g)

+

½ SERVE VEGETABLES

¼ cup cooked carrots, broccoli, pumpkin or spinach

OR

½ cup green leafy or raw vegetables

½ SERVE WHOLE GRAINS

¼ cup cooked rice, pasta, noodles or barley

OR

½ slice bread or ¼ medium roll or flatbread

OR

⅓ cup wheat cereal flakes or muesli

+

2½ SERVES VEGETABLES

1¼ cups cooked carrots, broccoli, pumpkin or spinach

OR

2½ cups green leafy or raw vegetables

Case study • Alexis

Alexis, a 33-year-old single mother of two children under five, works full-time in the hospitality industry. She had always tried to eat well, but over the last few years she had felt a nagging sense of tiredness. It seemed that no matter how much she tried to give herself a rest, the feeling just wouldn't lift. With a busy job and kids to care for, this mainly meant relaxing on the couch most nights once the jobs were done. Adjusting to life as a single parent hadn't been easy. The few glasses of wine each night started out as a little comforting treat but had actually become a hard habit to break.

The turning point came when she realised that, bit by bit, her clothes were getting tighter and just felt uncomfortable. She realised that she felt worse, not better, with all the 'relaxing' and 'treats' that she had at the end of the day. Although it seemed almost impossible to find the energy, she knew deep down that she needed to get off the couch and find a way to get active at home once her kids were in bed . . . and switch the wine for water a bit more often.

Alexis looked around on the internet for some exercise ideas and started week one by simply doing a set of stretches on the living room floor, followed by a herbal tea. Over time, this progressed to some strengthening moves, such as lunges and modified push ups. As she felt stronger, Alexis added some star jumps and running on the spot to get her heart rate up. Within the space of a few months, Alexis had grown to love that 30–60 minutes to move, stretch, get strong and do something 'for her'. It also helped to break the cycle of drinking wine every night – lemon water or herbal tea had become the norm for weeknights.

An unexpected benefit was better sleep, perhaps because of the increased activity, or reduced alcohol, and maybe even because she was looking at her phone less before bed. Overall, Alexis' energy levels were up, her clothes were back to being more comfortable and she found she was able to enjoy more quality time with her kids.

Case study • Roula

Roula was 53 years old with two teenage boys and had recently cut back to part-time work to help care for her ageing parents. At school, she had been a bit bigger than some of the other kids and she'd started to feel more self-conscious about her appearance as she got into her teenage years. In her early 20s, a friend suggested that they try to 'lose weight' together. Roula recalled that she lost weight and felt more in control of her eating habits, but she didn't become 'thin', as she had expected she would. Since then, she had tried every strategy that came along. Each experience had been the same – she would fall into the trap of eating something she wasn't supposed to, feel guilty, and then eat whatever she wanted to make herself feel better. She would then resolve to start all over again – usually on a Monday!

Roula was always feeling bad about herself – as though she had failed, rather than the approach failing her. With the emotional drain of her new caring responsibilities, she was exhausted from all the self-imposed guilt. She decided that she needed to break this cycle and change the way that she was thinking about herself, particularly now that she was post-menopausal.

Roula picked one change to make a start. Most nights, she was eating fairly mindlessly while cooking, cleaning up and watching TV. It dawned on her that she wasn't hungry to start with, and she wasn't really full afterwards either, so she worked towards changing this habit. She decided that she needed to sit at the table to eat with whoever was at home. That helped her to eat only at mealtimes, and more slowly.

Roula really enjoyed eating for the right reasons – nourishing her body when she felt the rumbly 'hungry' tummy and sharing healthy home-cooked meals with her family. Roula started to appreciate her body for what it could do rather than just how it looked. These changes boosted her self-belief in being able to take care of herself, not just others.

Menopause

Menopause refers to a woman's last menstrual period. It marks the time when ovulation ceases, levels of oestrogen and progesterone fall and becoming pregnant is no longer possible. Menopause usually occurs between the ages of 45 and 55 years, but can take place earlier or later.

The time leading up to menopause is called perimenopause. During this time, you will often start experiencing changes in your menstrual cycle, such as less regular or lighter periods. The changes in hormone levels can also cause physical and psychological changes.

Common symptoms of perimenopause include hot flushes and night sweats, muscle aches, dry skin, dry vagina, lower sex-drive and sleeping difficulties. Not every woman will experience these, and about two-thirds of women will have mild symptoms.

Hormonal changes, together with sleep deprivation, can also contribute to emotional and mood changes, anxiety, irritability, forgetfulness and trouble concentrating or making decisions.

Perimenopause can last between 4 and 8 years. After you have had no periods for 12 consecutive months, you're considered to be postmenopausal.

While the list of symptoms might seem overwhelming, the good news is that they can be partly managed by eating well and continuing to move your body.

Are there foods I should focus on during menopause?

There are some specific food groups and nutrients that are beneficial during and after menopause:

▸ **FRUIT AND VEGETABLES** Eating plenty of fruit and vegetables is particularly important during and after menopause. These are packed with vitamins and minerals, fibre and antioxidants, and regular consumption has been shown to help to reduce hot flushes in some women.

▸ **OMEGA-3 FATS** Some, though not all, studies have suggested that omega-3 fats can help relieve the symptoms of menopause. This can be achieved through regular fish consumption, or dietary supplements.

▸ **LOW-GI FOODS** These can help lower blood sugar levels, and eating these foods rather than sugary alternatives can help reduce hot flushes (see page 66).

▸ **PHYTOESTROGENS** These plant compounds occur naturally in many foods, but especially in soybeans, tofu, chickpeas, flaxseeds and black tea. These foods act as weak oestrogens in our bodies. There has been some controversy about whether these help or hinder women during menopause. Reviews of high-quality research suggests they may have some health benefits, along with possibly protecting against heart disease.

▸ **LEAN MEAT, EGGS AND DAIRY** These provide protein and calcium to help prevent muscle loss and support bone health, both of which become important during and after menopause.

Sleep

The quality and quantity of sleep we get changes over our lifetime, partly influenced by natural changes in our body clock. The effects of poor sleep can creep up over time and affect our wellbeing. If you think this is affecting you, consider whether any of these factors might be at play: sleep apnoea, excessive need to go to the toilet, chronic pain, stress or anxiety, effects of alcohol consumption, lack of exercise, high caffeine intake and the effects of screen time before bed. Talk to your GP if you feel that your wellbeing is impacted by unsatisfactory sleep.

TAKE ACTION

Muscle mass declines with age and so increasing your intake of high-quality protein is important.

▶ Aim to eat around 20–25 g of protein at main meals (see page 68). See also *CSIRO Protein Plus* for more information.

▶ Stay active to maintain muscle mass, including doing resistance exercise. Given the hormonal make up of women, resistance exercises will make you stronger, but not 'bulky'. Examples include using hand weights, resistance bands or making your body work against its own weight (lunges, push ups and squats).

Are there foods I should avoid during menopause?

Caffeine and alcohol can contribute to hot flushes in some women. They also disrupt sleep – so it may be helpful to avoid or minimise these if you find you are having trouble sleeping, at least towards the end of the day. And while some women report that avoiding certain foods can help relieve their symptoms, the good news is that there is no evidence suggesting the need to avoid any healthy foods.

Changing body size and shape after menopause

Many people are quick to blame hormones for weight gain that is common after menopause, but there is no known direct link. There are several changes that occur around this stage of life, which can have an effect on body shape and size:

- ◉ We tend to exercise less in our forties, fifties and sixties than when we are younger, which contributes to a decrease in muscle mass. Muscle mass helps burn energy, so less muscle mass means we need less food to maintain the same weight.

- ◉ Our lifestyles change. This may include eating more because of an unstructured lifestyle that comes with working less or retirement.

- ◉ Alcohol consumption increases with age, and adds to energy intake.

- ◉ Lower oestrogen levels during and after menopause promotes fat storage around your waist, so you might find your body shape changing accordingly.

Case Study • Margo

Margo, a 62-year-old woman, had never experienced any major health issues, but since going through menopause she was feeling really tired all the time.

A friend had told her that it was normal for energy levels to change after menopause, but Margo wasn't convinced. Worried that there might be something wrong with her thyroid gland (since she thought that thyroid problems can slow down your metabolism), she went to her GP.

After her thyroid hormone tests came back normal, the doctor suggested that Margo attend some sessions with a physiotherapist to work out an activity plan together. The physio also explained the importance of eating enough protein to feed her muscles. Margo started to eat more dairy foods and lean meat, and also began experimenting with incorporating beans and lentils into her meals.

Margo learned about the importance of resistance exercise for maintaining her muscle mass and preventing frailty later in life. She'd never been a fan of going to the gym, but bought some hand weights and exercise bands, and found some great online classes that she could do in her own home. Her energy levels went up and she was feeling fitter and healthier than she had for years – even before menopause!

Reducing the risk of lifestyle diseases

In countries like Australia, people are living longer lives compared to just a few generations ago. This is thanks to better nutrition, cleaner drinking water, antibiotics and vaccines, sterilisation, safer childbirth and safer work environments. What's more, Australian women have a longer life expectancy than men – typically living about two and half years longer.

Yet more and more of us are living with so-called lifestyle diseases. These long-term, chronic conditions have now become the leading cause of ill health, disability and death in Australia and many other countries. Australian data shows that women have a higher disease burden than men due to the fact that they are living with these diseases for longer.

It's true that genes play a part in determining our likelihood of developing these diseases. Some individuals, families and ethnic populations have genetic profiles that increase the risk of certain chronic diseases, and genes cannot be modified. Earlier in this book, we described other risk factors we can't change, such as our birthweight (see page 36). However, there are a lot of factors that we *can* change. If you do have any of the so-called 'non-modifiable' risk factors, it doesn't mean you will end up with a disease – but it does make healthy eating and lifestyle choices even more important.

COMMON LIFESTYLE DISEASES AFFECTING AUSTRALIAN WOMEN*

- cardiovascular diseases (such as coronary heart disease, vascular disease and stroke);
- type 2 diabetes;
- certain cancers;
- respiratory diseases, including asthma and chronic obstructive pulmonary disease;
- osteoarthritis;
- osteoporosis;
- chronic kidney disease.

*Mental health disorders (as a general term to describe a broad spectrum of conditions) are appropriately receiving recognition as a significant and common chronic disease. However, mental health conditions do not have the same underlying modifiable risk factors as physical conditions, and require a different and specialised approach to management, treatment and prevention.

Half of all Australian females report having one or more of these chronic conditions. This rate increases with age.

43%
OF WOMEN AGED 45 YEARS AND OVER REPORT HAVING AT LEAST ONE CHRONIC DISEASE.

83%
OF WOMEN AGED 65 YEARS AND OVER REPORT HAVING AT LEAST ONE CHRONIC DISEASE.

EARLY WARNING SIGNS

The measurable early warning signs for risk of developing a chronic disease include:

- high blood pressure;
- high cholesterol levels;
- high blood sugar and insulin levels;
- high markers of inflammation;
- high BMI and/or waist circumference.

It is important to have regular health checks with your GP and participate in national screening programs (such as Breast Screen Australia, National Bowel Cancer Screening Program and the National Cervical Screening Program). Regular health checks may cover heart health, type 2 diabetes risk, eye health, bone health, and checking the size and shape of moles or freckles.

This will alert you to any early warning signs that you are at increased risk of developing one or more of these lifestyle diseases. It is a chance to monitor your health and, if needed, make lifestyle changes to turn things around.

COMMON CAUSES

Many people develop more than one of these chronic diseases, mainly because the diseases share similar causes related to lifestyle behaviours. The four main lifestyle-related causes for chronic disease that can be modified are:

- physical inactivity;
- unhealthy eating habits;
- smoking;
- harmful use of alcohol.

And here is the good news – if key lifestyle behaviours are improved, the risk of developing a multitude of chronic diseases, and the progression of those conditions, can be substantially reduced.

TAKING ACTION

The key message is simple and backed up by strong scientific evidence – by eating well and leading an active life, along with not smoking and limiting or avoiding alcohol, you will go a long way to looking after your health and protecting yourself from lifestyle diseases. It's never too early or too late to change bad habits and replace them with healthier habits. If you already have one of these conditions, making lifestyle changes will also have huge health benefits.

Check your salt

On average, Australians consume nearly double the recommended amount of salt. Eating too much salt can lead to high blood pressure, a risk factor for heart disease.

One of the best ways to reduce salt intake is to eat mainly fresh, unprocessed foods. Most of the salt we consume comes from processed and packaged foods. Tastebuds adjust, so just as we become used to highly salted foods, we also get used to less salty foods. When cooking, add flavour with herbs, spices, nuts and healthy dressings rather than salt.

CHRONIC DISEASES

In addition to the four main lifestyle factors that help prevent all chronic diseases (see page 61), research has pinpointed some other lifestyle factors that can help reduce the risk of specific chronic diseases.

Cardiovascular diseases

Cardiovascular disease remains one of the leading causes of death in Australia. In addition to the general guidelines of eating well and staying active, the National Heart Foundation has some specific nutritional recommendations:

- Eating plenty of vegetables and fruit will help to keep blood vessels healthy.
- Fibre from wholegrains can help to lower blood cholesterol levels.
- Aim for 2–3 serves of oily fish per week.
- If you eat red meat, have no more than 455 g (cooked weight) lean red meat per week.
- If you have heart disease or high cholesterol, reduced-fat milk, yoghurt and cheese are better choices than full-fat varieties.
- Include healthy oils such as olive, canola, sunflower, peanut, sesame and safflower, along with unsalted nuts, seeds, avocados and olives.
- Use herbs and spices for flavour, instead of salt.

Osteoporosis

Women are at particular risk of developing osteoporosis after menopause because of the reduction in oestrogen levels. Lower oestrogen levels cause faster loss of calcium and other minerals from bones. If you are aged over 50 years, speak to your GP about whether a bone-density scan is necessary.

Some specific recommendations to maintain bone health throughout life include:

- Aim for 3–5 serves of calcium-rich food daily, with the number of serves depending on the level of calcium in each food (see page 71 for detailed information on calcium-rich foods).
- Include dairy products (or fortified dairy alternatives): these foods are the richest source of calcium, as well as other nutrients that are important for bone health, like potassium and magnesium.
- Ensure you are getting enough vitamin D from foods, sunlight or supplements (see below).
- Regular bone strengthening activities that involve weight-bearing are also important for achieving and maintaining bone health.

Vitamin D and bone health

Vitamin D helps to absorb calcium from food, regulate calcium levels in the blood, and support growth and maintenance of the skeleton. Food cannot provide an adequate amount of vitamin D and most people are reliant on sun exposure to reach recommended levels – it is produced when our skin is exposed to sunlight. The amount of sun exposure needed is low and can be achieved while avoiding the risk of skin damage. In summer, most Australian adults will maintain adequate levels during day-to-day outdoor activities (remembering sun protection). In winter, longer exposure times are needed. For people with low vitamin D levels, a supplement may be required.

Cancers

Smoking tobacco is the leading preventable cause of all cancers. However, there are many different types of cancer, and some have specific risk factors:

- Alcohol consumption increases the risk of developing cancers of the bowel, mouth, pharynx, larynx, oesophagus, liver and breast. The risk increases relative to the amount of alcohol consumed, but even drinking small amounts increases risk.

- Excessive sun exposure and use of solariums increase the risk of skin cancer. Follow sun-smart principles, including wearing sunscreen and protective clothing, and have your skin checked regularly.

- Eating plenty of plant-based foods, including fruit, vegetables and other foods containing dietary fibre, may protect against certain cancers.

- Avoiding processed meats, such as cured meats, sausages and bacon, and limiting red meat may protect against some cancers (see page 68 for more on red meat).

- Viral infections such as the human papillomavirus (HPV) or chronic infection with the hepatitis B or C viruses increases the risk of certain cancers. Vaccination can protect against the human HPV and hepatitis B. Protective behaviours, such as safe sex, can reduce the risk of hepatitis C.

Brain health

The brain is an outstandingly important and complex organ, responsible for keeping our body functioning, movement, speech, memory, feelings and so much more. There are some changes in the brain that occur over the course of life that are considered normal. These may make us slower to remember a person's name or occasionally forget an appointment.

However, there are also age-related brain conditions that are more serious and can have a major impact on our quality of life.

Dementia is a term that describes a number of conditions affecting the brain that are not a normal part of ageing and are due to progressive deterioration in its functioning. This includes conditions such as Alzheimer's disease.

A healthy lifestyle is important for maintaining brain health and can help to reduce the risk of dementia later in life. Lifestyle factors that appear to increase the risk of dementia include inadequate physical activity, unhealthy eating habits, cardiovascular disease and related conditions, poor sleep quality, social isolation and depression. Recent research also shows an important link between brain health and heart and blood vessel health. Avoiding smoking, limiting or avoiding alcohol, and maintaining normal blood pressure and cholesterol levels and a healthy weight can all support brain health.

PART TWO

turning plans

plans

Invest in yourself

We all want to be healthy and happy. Many women strive to fit eating well and regular movement into their busy lives. Both social and mainstream media outlets have latched onto these good intentions and as a result, they can overload us with confusing (and often inaccurate) information about our health and the way we 'should' eat.

But the expectation to have a 'perfect' lifestyle and eating habits doesn't just come from the media. Our peers, family, friends, social norms and even so-called influencers can also place both overt and subtle pressures on women. The common portrayal of unrealistic female bodies places undue pressure on many women to look a certain way and have a certain body shape. All of these pressures can dampen our self-esteem and self-confidence, which in turn negatively impacts both our mind and our body.

A more positive approach is to think about how we can nourish our bodies by eating a balanced, wholesome and enjoyable variety of foods.

Restrictive eating trends

Women are constantly exposed to new eating trends – sugar-free, paleo, fasting and 'clean' eating to name a few. These approaches may recommend restrictions on how much we eat (such as counting kilojoules), when we eat (such as skipping meals) or what we eat (such as avoiding major food groups). For further discussion about these, see page 25.

Following the latest eating trend has become so ingrained that some women don't notice the habit both in thinking and actions. Whether the goal is the pursuit of better health or a different body shape, becoming overly restrictive with what we eat is becoming increasingly common.

Typically, these short-lived attempts to change how or what we eat do little to actually improve our health. For example, if we cut out whole food groups, we can miss out on important nutrients. An inadequate intake of essential nutrients over time can affect mood and energy levels and increase vulnerability to illness.

Restrictive or extreme eating patterns have been shown to increase feelings of guilt about eating and deflate our body image. And since these approaches are usually difficult to stick to, we inevitably experience a sense of 'failure' and the letdown of not 'doing it right' when things don't go according to plan. Over time, this can reduce our belief that we can make a positive difference to our health.

Habits: hurting or helping our health?

Habits are daily behaviours that become increasingly automatic when we engage in them in the same place and at the same time each day. We tend to lack awareness of our automatic behaviours and, once established, habits can be difficult to break.

Habits can allow us to do things without thinking about them too much, such as brushing our teeth. This can save us time and mental energy, which we can all agree are precious resources in today's world. But some habits do not serve us or our health so well. For example, do you find yourself reaching for a snack as soon as you step through the door after work? Every time you reach for a snack (behaviour) when you get home from work (cue), you strengthen the link. Eventually, getting home from work will prompt you to eat automatically, even if you are not hungry.

Forming new habits

The evidence-based approach outlined opposite will help to break and change unwanted habits, and turn new, positive behaviours into habits that are geared towards a healthier lifestyle. This approach works best when you:

- focus on changing one thing at a time;
- are realistic about the scale of change – aim for small and incremental changes;
- allow enough time for that new change to become a habit before moving on to another change – trying to overhaul too much at once is a recipe for failure;
- are supported by family and friends.

Sharing habits

We learn habits from the world and the people around us, including our parents, family, peers and the media. We can also pass our own habits onto our family, friends and colleagues. Reflect on these questions:

- What habits have you learned from others that have helped you to make healthier lifestyle choices?
- What habits have you learned from others that you want to change?
- Which of your own habits do you want to model to your family, friends or children to promote health and wellbeing?

DISRUPT AN UNHEALTHY HABIT

1 SELF-MONITOR YOUR HABITS

To change your habit, you need to know more about it. This can be a challenge, as automatic behaviours often go unnoticed, but it can be achieved by keeping a record of your habit (e.g. night-time snacking). Record how often (e.g. daily) and when it occurs (e.g. after work), as well as what else is happening (e.g. feeling stressed).

2 DISRUPT THE ENVIRONMENT

A key starting point is to become familiar with the environmental cues or situations that automatically trigger unwanted habits.

Try to reduce exposure to the cues or environments that reinforce your habit (e.g. stop stocking the tempting night-time snacks in the cupboard and instead place a bowl of fresh fruit on the counter). Environmental cues can also change naturally via our life transitions, such as when we move to a new house, change jobs, move in with or separate from a partner, have children or when our kids leave home. For example, you may find that starting a new job provides you with an opportunity to cycle to work instead of taking the train. Make the most of change to disrupt an old habit and start a new healthy one!

3 MANAGE CHALLENGING SITUATIONS

You might find you 'slip up' and perform an old habit when you are distracted. Acknowledge the emotional or social triggers of your unwanted habit but then remind yourself of your goals. Try to be mindful of the impact of stress and go easy on yourself when you are not perfect. The key is to not give up after a setback – it happens to all of us!

CREATE A NEW HEALTHY HABIT

1 SMALL CHANGES

Decide on one new habit that you would like to develop to boost your health and wellbeing.

2 MAKE IT SMART: SPECIFIC, MEASURABLE, ACHIEVABLE, REALISTIC AND TIMEBOUND

Choose a simple action you can do routinely that will move you towards achieving your new healthy habit. Keeping it specific and manageable makes you more likely to succeed and making it timebound gives you a deadline.

3 PLAN FOR SUCCESS AND CREATE A SUPPORTIVE ENVIRONMENT

Remove triggers for old habits (e.g. a lolly jar on your desk or a packet of chips in your pantry at home) and think about alternative, healthier habits (e.g. keep running shoes under your desk, bring a refillable water bottle to work).

4 SAME TIME, SAME PLACE

Decide when and where you will do your chosen action and be consistent.

5 REPETITION IS KEY

Repeat the action every time you come across that time and place.

6 STICK WITH IT

Take advantage of knowing how habits develop and use this to build a better habit. It will get easier with time. Most people find that they start doing the action without even thinking about it within about 10 weeks, give or take.

NEW HABITS FOR HEALTH

It is important that the food we eat nourishes our body. In addition, the way we eat and the physical activity we do should also be pleasurable, social and consistent with our personal preferences, priorities, culture and beliefs. Are there changes you want to make? Spend time reflecting on what, how, why, when and where you eat or do the activity that you want to change. Allow time for that new change to become a habit before moving on to another change. Use these tables to help you think about and plan how you might establish a new healthy lifestyle habit.

Examples of healthy eating and activity habits

DO MORE

WHAT	HOW	WHERE	WHEN	WHY
Making a bit more time to prepare delicious, healthy food; walking short distances instead of taking the car.	Taking the time to enjoy eating a meal; taking the stairs instead of the lift.	Sitting outside to eat lunch; eating a relaxed dinner at the dining table with the kids; stretching while watching TV.	Starting the day with a healthy breakfast; walking around the block at lunchtime.	Eating when hungry or to 'fuel' my body for a boost of energy; because I deserve to nourish my body with nutritious food; being active as a way to connect with family or friends.

DO LESS

WHAT	HOW	WHERE	WHEN	WHY
Finishing off the children's food; unrestrained snacking; going back for extra; watching an extra episode rather than having a quick walk.	Rushing meals, eating too quickly; stopping when a bit puffed.	Sitting at the desk for lunch; eating while watching TV; eating when driving; staying in bed rather than getting up a bit earlier to do some activity.	Skipping breakfast; eating late at night; snacking between meals; working through lunch.	Needing a 'treat' when bored, tired or stressed; feeling guilty or regretting what I ate; exercising to 'work off' or 'earn' food; putting off activity because it seems too hard.

Allow time for a new change to become a habit before moving on to another change

STEPS FOR CHANGING BEHAVIOURS	EXAMPLE	YOUR BEHAVIOUR CHANGE
Reflect on your lifestyle to decide on a specific aspect to change and understand the triggers.	I've noticed that I've started buying soft drinks when my workmates and I take a quick afternoon walk. Once I start, it's hard to switch back to drinking water.	
Set a Specific, Measurable, Achievable, Realistic, Timebound goal.	During the week, I will switch my regular soft drink for a kombucha, which I can also buy from the shop on our walk.	
Plan for success.	I will clear out any soft drinks from my pantry at home. If I can't find a kombucha, I'll try a mineral water.	
Monitor your progress.	I will track my new healthy behaviour via the Notes app in my phone.	
Deploy strategies to bounce back when things don't go according to plan.	Once the weather starts to get colder, I might slip into the habit of buying a hot chocolate. If this happens, I will switch it for herbal tea.	

Healthy habits for life

Being active, eating well, limiting alcohol and not smoking are habits that are best formed early and kept for life.

These key habits reduce the risk of many common chronic diseases (see page 48). While it can be hard to prioritise bone or heart health in your twenties, when you reach your seventies, you may be grateful for a lifetime of eating well and being active. There are short-term benefits, too, such as improved concentration and more energy.

1 MOVE YOUR BODY – AND HAVE SOME FUN DOING IT!

Switch staying on the couch for something that will really stimulate your body's feel-good neurochemicals. Being active doesn't need to be exhausting to be effective. Simply moving your body in a way that you enjoy will have benefits, and doing any physical activity is better than doing none. It's great for your heart, bones, muscles, energy levels, balance, posture, flexibility, sleep and mind. Try to:

- Be active on most, preferably all, days of the week.
- Enjoy a variety of activities that boost your fitness, flexibility and strength.
- Gradually build up to 2.5 to 5 hours of moderate-intensity physical activity (at a level where you can still talk comfortably) or 1.25 to 2.5 hours of vigorous-intensity physical activity (at a level where you can just say a few words) each week.

If you are starting a new activity, begin at a level that is easily manageable, then gradually build up the amount, type and frequency. Try these ideas to start:

- Walk with the kids, dog, partner or neighbour.
- Get out in the garden: it is not just the physical activity that helps – being in nature has been shown to offer relief for many things from negative feelings through to depression.
- Use housework as an opportunity to move: pop in earphones and find a podcast you enjoy.
- Play music and dance like nobody's watching – enjoy those feel-good neurochemicals flooding your body.
- Find a workout app or device that suits your need, whether it's a free 7-minute at-home workout, a step tracker, or online yoga classes.
- Do some stretches – there are lots of great guides online.

Walking and jogging are good for the leg muscles and bone – but don't forget about strong arms. Talk to a physiotherapist or qualified personal trainer about some simple at-home exercises you can slot into your day.

Also, remember that exercise doesn't have to be done only once a day. Some people will find it easier to do a number of bouts of 5, 10 or 15 minutes spread across the day.

2 NOURISH YOUR BODY – THE HABIT OF EATING WELL

Eating well is not an 'all or nothing' dichotomy, and it doesn't need to be complicated or in pursuit of perfection. Lead with balanced and sensible portion sizes. Don't be hard on yourself about the occasional treat, especially if you're eating mostly healthy foods each day. Allow yourself to enjoy the occasional indulgence but be realistic about how much and how often you are enjoying them.

The six core food groups

The foundation of eating mostly unprocessed foods from the six core food groups has stood the test of time. The way we eat will undoubtedly change over the course of our lifetime, but these foundations should underpin each of those different phases and stages. Enjoy the appropriate amount of these foods to maintain a healthy weight for you, and drink mainly water.

Choose foods from these six core groups:

- plenty of vegetables, including different types and colours, and legumes
- fruit
- grain (cereal) foods, mostly wholegrain and/or high-fibre varieties
- lean meat and poultry, fish, eggs, tofu, nuts and seeds, and legumes
- milk, yoghurt, cheese and/or their alternatives
- healthy oils and fats.

There are many ways to combine these foods in healthy and balanced ways. Different cuisines, cultures, religious customs, personal preferences and lifestyle demands can be accommodated.

It is true that having a high BMI is a risk factor for the development of many diseases. Weight loss is often recommended as a strategy to reduce disease risk. This can be achieved gradually and maintained through healthy eating habits that are in balance with activity levels. The support and personalised dietary advice of an Accredited Practising Dietitian can help to make this an achievable target.

Remember that the aim is not to look a certain way or be a certain size, but rather to achieve your best health through eating well, being active, limiting or avoiding alcohol and not smoking. Strong scientific evidence has shown that there are many health benefits from achieving and sustaining just a 5 per cent reduction in weight if you have a high BMI, regardless of whether that then puts your weight into the healthy range.

3 REDUCE THE HEALTH RISKS LINKED TO DRINKING ALCOHOL

Unlike the many different ways to 'eat well', there is a lot less ambiguity when it comes alcohol. In fact, the evidence about the harmful effects of alcohol is becoming stronger.

The latest Australian recommendations state that to reduce the risk of harm from alcohol-related disease or injury, you should drink no more than 10 standard drinks per week and no more than 4 standard drinks on any one day. The less you choose to drink, the lower your risk of alcohol-related harm. If you choose to drink, limit your intake.

Some people may find their alcohol intake is difficult to manage, and not drinking at all might be the safest option. If you want to stop drinking alcohol, it's a good idea to see your GP who can help you to develop an action plan with goals, strategies and a support network. They can also consider the likelihood of alcohol withdrawal symptoms and how they can be managed.

Children and young people under 18 years of age should not drink alcohol. To reduce the risk of harm to their unborn child, women who are pregnant or planning a pregnancy should not drink alcohol. For women who are breastfeeding, not drinking alcohol is safest for their baby. If putting this into practice feels hard, refer to our guide to disrupting healthy habits (page 57).

4 DON'T SMOKE – AND IF YOU DO, SEEK SUPPORT TO QUIT

Like alcohol, the evidence for tobacco smoking is unarguable. The chemicals in tobacco smoke are addictive and toxic. Tobacco smoke causes harmful effects throughout the body and increases the risk of cancer and other diseases. It is also important to avoid second-hand exposure to smoke from other people's cigarettes and tobacco products, especially for unborn babies, children and people with breathing problems.

Quitting smoking is hard: icanquit.com.au provides advice for quitting smoking, and you can also get support from your GP.

Focus on nourishing your body, rather than depriving it, by eating well and being active.

Eating well: benefits of the core food groups

This chapter provides more detail about the core food groups, answers some questions and clears up some common misconceptions. We outline the core elements of eating well for health through an approach that is sensible, easy to follow, and will serve you well across all stages of life.

Because this book focuses on developing and maintaining healthy lifelong eating habits, there is little emphasis on quantities, limits and 'don'ts'.

You are on the right track for overall health and wellbeing if you:

- mostly choose foods and drinks that are from the core food groups;
- limit discretionary food – those foods and drinks that contain alcohol, added sugar, or are high in saturated fat or salt, or are highly processed and lacking in beneficial nutrients.

VEGETABLES

An eating plan that contains plenty of vegetables and lots of variety can provide a range of beneficial nutrients. About 95 per cent of women do not meet the recommended intake of 5 serves of vegetables every day, which means they are missing out on the vitamins, minerals and dietary fibre that vegetables provide.

People who have at least three different vegetables in their dinner every day are more likely to have a healthier eating pattern overall.

KEY POINTS

- The more colour on your plate, the better.
- Choose low- and no-salt canned or frozen vegetables as a convenient alternative.
- Choose seasonal whenever possible.
- Don't forget to include legumes such as chickpeas, black beans, lentils and kidney beans.
- Eat more veggies more often by thinking of creative ways to include them at breakfast and lunch, as well as dinner, and as a healthy between-meal snack.

Get more veggies into your day

+ Have some cut-up veggies stored in airtight containers in the fridge ready for an easy snack.

+ Do your kids have a tendency to snack just before dinner is ready? As you are chopping up veggies for dinner, put some aside for the kids (and you) to munch on.

+ Rethink peeling veggies – often a wash or scrub is adequate. You will save both time and nutrients.

+ Have a pot of vegetable soup ready for when the afternoon munchies hit.

+ Add a side salad to meals.

+ Add extra veggies to your stews, casseroles, pasta sauces and curries.

+ Have some veggies in your breakfast – baked beans or mushrooms on toast is a quick and healthy start to the day.

FRUIT

While we are more likely to meet the fruit (2 a day) than the vegetable (5 a day) recommendation, we still have a way to go.

To get more fruit into your day:

- Cut up some fruit and store it in an airtight container in the fridge to grab when you feel a mid-afternoon hunger pang.
- Stock up on frozen fruit to add to smoothies and healthy desserts.
- Replenish your fruit bowl regularly.
- Squeeze some citrus, such as lemon or lime, or even pineapple juice, on cut apples, bananas, pears and peaches to prevent them from going brown.

KEY POINTS

- ▶ The more variety, the better.
- ▶ Whole fruit is a better choice than juice, dried or rolled fruit because it has more fibre and less sugar.
- ▶ Choose seasonal whenever possible for better value and quality.
- ▶ Choose canned fruit in 'natural juice' rather than 'syrup', as an occasional alternative to fresh fruit.

GRAIN (CEREAL) FOODS

Most of the carbohydrate-based foods you choose should be wholegrain. Wholegrains retain the outer husk and bran layer, so as well as being a great source of fibre, they provide a multitude of nutrients, including folate and other B vitamins. They are also more filling and give the body an even spread of energy.

Glycaemic index (GI) – is it worth paying attention to?

The glycaemic index is a way that carbohydrates in foods and drinks are ranked according to how quickly they raise blood sugar levels. Foods with a low GI are a better choice because they take longer for the carbohydrate to be digested and absorbed. Not only does this slow the rate that glucose enters the blood circulation, it also keeps us feeling full for longer.

The GI is an excellent way to guide the selection of carbohydrate-containing foods. Choosing lower-GI foods is a healthy approach for everyone, but especially for people with type 2 diabetes (and those at risk of developing diabetes) to assist with managing their blood sugar levels.

It's important to remember that many non-grain foods – including dairy, fruit, legumes and some vegetables (including potato, corn and pumpkin) – also contain carbohydrates and have a GI. Sometimes the GI ranking can seem a little confusing. For example, some types of fruit can have a higher GI than some discretionary foods such as biscuits, but fruit is still the healthier choice – it is higher in beneficial nutrients and fibre.

The amount of the carbohydrate-containing food you eat also has an important influence on blood sugar levels. For example, pasta may have a low GI, but if you consume a large serving, this will cause your blood glucose levels to rise more. So in this case, serving less pasta, but loading up on a vegetable-rich sauce and a side salad would be a healthier choice.

In summary, the glycaemic index can help guide your food choices, but it might be just as helpful to remember that the less processed, the better. Always aim to balance the carbohydrate with other core food groups.

The longer it takes to digest and absorb breads, cereals and other grains, the better.

KEY POINTS

▶ Bread and crackers/crispbreads: choose wholegrain, wholemeal, rye or high-fibre white bread. Choose the wholemeal or wholegrain versions of rolls, English muffins, crumpets, pita, flatbreads and mountain breads.

▶ Rice: try brown, wild, black or red rice varieties. Basmati and Doongara are good options too, as they have a lower GI.

▶ Pasta and noodles: choose wholemeal where possible, or start by using wholemeal options some of the time.

▶ Flour: choose wholemeal where possible, or a combination of half white and half wholemeal flour.

Get more fibre from your grains

+ Look for the word 'whole' in the title of breads: wholegrain or wholemeal breads, crispbreads and rolls.

+ Look for the word 'bran' when choosing your breakfast cereals.

+ Experiment with oats as they are full of fibre. Try the Oat and apple bowl for breaky (see page 93) or the Strawberry Crumble for dessert (see page 224).

+ Try other grains, such as freekeh, quinoa, couscous, polenta, pearl barley and burghul (cracked wheat).

LEAN MEAT, FISH AND ALTERNATIVES

This food group includes animal and plant sources of dietary protein: chicken, pork, turkey, beef, lamb, seafood, eggs, legumes, tofu and plant-based mince such as Quorn™. Different protein-containing foods offer a range of protein types that are digested and absorbed by the body differently.

These foods also provide a variety of other beneficial nutrients such as iron, zinc, omega-3 fats and vitamin B12. Foods from other core food groups also provide some protein. Dairy foods are a source of protein, along with other nutrients such as calcium. Nuts and seeds contain protein, along with healthy oils. Legumes provide protein, along with carbohydrate and fibre.

Processed meats such as ham, cured meats and bacon should be avoided, or only eaten occasionally, because they can be high in saturated fats and salt.

Dietary protein:

- helps build and maintain muscle mass and strength, when combined with resistance exercises;

- helps with weight management by regulating appetite;

- promotes healthy ageing. Combining resistance exercise with adequate protein intake prevents the muscle loss that happens as we get older. This is important for retaining physical strength and independence.

How much protein do you need?

Our body's requirement for protein varies at different life stages. For women, protein needs are highest during childhood and adolescence, as well as during pregnancy and breastfeeding. The Australian recommended dietary intakes (RDIs) for protein are a daily average of 0.75 grams of protein for each kilogram of body weight for women 19–70 years of age. However, recent research and expert committees conclude that healthy adults might benefit from a higher daily average protein intake of between 1.2 to 1.6 grams of protein for each kilogram of body weight. The recipes in this book provide enough protein from a variety of sources to cover this higher protein range for most people (when breakfast, lunch and dinner recipes are combined across a day's eating), noting that protein also comes from multiple food groups.

Let's take a look at an example. **Samara** weighs 70 kg. What does 1.2–1.6 grams of protein per kilogram of bodyweight look like for her?

1.2 G (OF PROTEIN) X 70 KG (BODY WEIGHT)	1.6 G (OF PROTEIN) X 70 KG (BODY WEIGHT)
=84 GRAMS OF PROTEIN	**=112** GRAMS OF PROTEIN

So Samara should aim for approximately 84–112 grams of protein per day.

The table opposite is an example of Samara's eating habits and shows how she would achieve a protein intake in this range. She has spread her protein intake fairly evenly across the day, which allows the body to make the best use of the dietary protein. Aim for about 25 g of protein per main meal. This is equivalent to about 100 g raw lean meat. The main meal recipes in this book provide about this amount of protein per serve.

SAMARA'S USUAL DAILY PROTEIN INTAKE

MEAL	FOOD	PROTEIN (GRAMS)
BREAKFAST	Breakfast cereal (30 g)	3
	Yoghurt (100 g)	7
	Milk (½ cup)	5
	Milky coffee (1 cup)	10
	Total breakfast	25
LUNCH	Tuna (100 g)	22
	Salad	<1
	Cheese (1 slice)	5
	Crispbread	3
	Total lunch	30
AFTERNOON TEA	Nuts (14 nuts)	3
DINNER	Chicken (150 g raw)	33
	Rice (½ cup cooked)	2
	Vegetables	1–6
	Total dinner	36–41
	TOTAL	94–99

A note on iron

Iron is an important nutrient for women because we are particularly at risk of iron deficiency. Women need twice as much iron as men in their reproductive years due to blood losses during menstruation and extra demands during pregnancy. Many Australian women don't meet their dietary iron requirements as a result of eating fewer iron-rich foods than men. A lack of iron can result in lack of energy and poor stamina. As well as meat and seafood sources, iron is found in legumes, tofu, green leafy vegetables, dried fruit, nuts, seeds and wholegrain foods, but at lower levels.

Get enough protein each day

+ Increase your protein at breakfast by adding foods such as milk, yoghurt, eggs and legumes. Typically, breakfasts are high in carbohydrate, such as cereal and toast.
+ Aim for plenty of variety. Add more fish dishes to your regular rotation of meals. Try some plant-based protein sources, such as tofu, and experiment with recipes containing legumes.

+ To get the same amount of dietary protein, a larger volume of plant-based proteins is needed compared to meat, fish, eggs, etc.
+ Remember to trim fat and remove the skin from animal meats because these are high in unhealthy saturated fat.

DAIRY AND ALTERNATIVES

Dairy-based foods such as milk, yoghurt and cheese provide calcium and protein (along with many other nutrients) that are important for building and maintaining strong and healthy bones. Calcium is easily absorbed from dairy foods and reduced-fat dairy options have the same amount of calcium as full-fat varieties. Dairy-based foods provide some saturated fat, which can raise cholesterol levels. If you have elevated blood cholesterol or heart disease, it is best to choose reduced-fat options. For everyone else, the evidence suggests that it is fine to choose the dairy foods you most enjoy. Choosing unflavoured milk and yoghurt will help avoid added sugars.

If you need or choose to avoid dairy products, make a habit of replacing them with calcium-fortified and unsweetened alternatives such as soy, rice or nut/cereal milks (e.g. almond or oat milk) and include plenty of other non-dairy calcium-rich foods, listed in the table opposite.

Why is calcium so important and how much do I need?

Nearly three-quarters of Australian women don't consume enough calcium. This is problematic because a regular supply of calcium is important for maintaining bone density.

Our calcium needs increase as we get older. Women aged 19–50 years need 1000 mg of calcium and women aged over 50 years need 1300 mg to prevent conditions including osteoporosis (see page 50). Use the table opposite as a guide to meeting your calcium needs.

MYTH

Regular milk is high in fat.

FACT

Regular milk is not a high-fat food. It has an average of 3.5 per cent fat. Reduced-fat milk usually has about 1.2 per cent fat and contains slightly less energy (kilojoules).

MYTH

Milk is a trigger for asthma.

FACT

There is no evidence that dairy products are a trigger for asthma. In fact, the Asthma Foundation recommends dairy as part of a healthy eating pattern.

Get enough calcium

+ Aim for at least 3 serves of dairy foods each day (e.g. 1 cup milk, 40 g (2 slices) cheese and 200 g yoghurt).
+ Try fish with small bones, such as canned salmon or sardines in your sandwich.
+ Include meals with tofu (try some of the delicious recipes in this book).
+ Choose almonds as between-meal snacks.
+ Choose breakfast cereals that are fortified with calcium.
+ Be adventurous with the variety of veggies, and choose collard greens, broccoli, mustard cabbage, bok choy, silverbeet, cucumber and celery.

THE CALCIUM CONTENT OF A SELECTION OF FOODS

FOOD GROUP	SERVE	APPROX. CALCIUM PER SERVE	ANYTHING ELSE I SHOULD KNOW?
DAIRY	1 cup milk, 200 g yoghurt, 40 g cheese	300 mg	Calcium-fortified versions have up to 400–500 mg per serve.
DAIRY ALTERNATIVES	1 cup calcium-fortified soy, rice, almond milk	300 mg	Always choose calcium-fortified versions. Calcium content will vary – check the Nutrition Information Panel on the labels.
TOFU	170 g	550 mg	Calcium content will vary – check the Nutrition Information Panel on the labels.
FISH	100 g tinned sardines or salmon	400 mg	Choose tinned fish with bones.
NUTS AND SEEDS	2 teaspoons nuts	40 mg	Choose almonds and Brazil nuts.
GREEN LEAFY VEGETABLES	1 cup cooked	100 mg	Absorption of calcium varies in all foods but can be as low as 5 per cent for some vegetables.
CALCIUM-FORTIFIED BREAKFAST CEREALS	⅔ cup	200 mg	Calcium content of fortified foods will vary – check the Nutrition Information Panel on the labels.

HEALTHY OILS AND FATS

When it comes to the impact of oils and fats on your health, it's as much (if not more!) about the quality as the quantity. The best approach to reduce the risk of lifestyle diseases such as type 2 diabetes and heart disease is to increase your intake of monounsaturated and polyunsaturated fats, especially omega-3 fats, and reduce intake of saturated and trans fats from foods such as pastries, biscuits, cakes, crisps, butter, cream and processed or untrimmed meats.

Many fats and oils are very healthy and should not be avoided. Their important roles in the body include carrying fat soluble vitamins, providing a structural component in cells and cushioning vital organs. They have essential roles in metabolic processes in the body. Omega-3 fatty acids, such as eicosapentaenoic acid (EPA) and docosahexaenoic acid (DHA), are associated with brain, bone, joint, eye and heart health benefits throughout life.

Aim to consume 2–3 servings of fish per week including fatty fish sources such as salmon, tuna, sardines and mackerel. Mussels are also a great source of omega-3 fats.

Fats and oils are energy dense and so it is helpful to be aware of quantities when trying to balance eating well with being active. If you use a spread, a thin scraping is all that is needed.

DID YOU KNOW THE EXTRACTION PROCESS USED TO PRODUCE EXTRA VIRGIN OLIVE OIL ENSURES IT RETAINS NUTRIENTS AND ANTIOXIDANTS FROM THE OLIVE FRUIT?

What's the deal with coconut oil?

There's been a lot of hype about the benefits of coconut oil. The reality is there is little scientific evidence to conclude that coconut oil is either healthy or harmful. When it comes to heart health, coconut oil raises both good (HDL) and bad (LDL) cholesterol. Increased consumption at the expense of other healthy fats is not recommended.

SEEDS ARE A DELICIOUS ADDITION TO BREAKFAST BOWLS, SALADS, SMOOTHIES, BREAD ...IN FACT, EVERYTHING!

CORE FOOD GROUPS

FOOD GROUP	SUGGESTED UNITS EACH DAY	WHAT'S A UNIT?	ANYTHING ELSE I SHOULD KNOW?
VEGETABLES	5 at least	▸ ½ cup cooked veggies ▸ 1 cup leafy or raw veggies	Variety and volume are the key. Fresh, frozen and tinned are all fine, but choose no-added-salt tinned options.
FRUIT	2–3	▸ 1 medium fruit e.g. apple ▸ 2 smaller fruits e.g. apricots ▸ 30 g dried fruit	Fresh fruit is best. Dried fruit and juice contain more sugar.
WHOLEGRAIN	5	▸ ½ cup cooked rice, pasta, noodles, quinoa or freekeh ▸ 1 slice of bread ▸ ⅔ cup high-fibre breakfast cereal	Choose wholegrain or wholemeal options. Starchy vegetables can be included in the 'grain' food group i.e. 150 g (1 medium) cooked potato or sweet potato.
DAIRY AND ALTERNATIVES	3 at least	▸ 1 cup milk or calcium-fortified dairy alternative ▸ 200 g yoghurt ▸ 40 g cheese	Choose low-fat if you have high cholesterol or heart disease. Unsweetened nut and grain milk alternatives should be calcium fortified.
LEAN MEAT, FISH AND ALTERNATIVES	2.5	▸ 100 g (raw weight) chicken, fish, beef, pork, turkey, lamb, Quorn™ ▸ 2 eggs ▸ 150 g cooked or tinned legumes ▸ 170 g tofu	Choose lean cuts of meat and trim off excess fat. Avoid processed meats, such as cured meats, sausages and bacon. Aim for 2–3 serves of fish each week.
HEALTHY OILS AND FATS	6	▸ 1 teaspoon oil or margarine ▸ 20 g avocado ▸ 2 teaspoons nuts/seeds	Choose unsaturated fats and oils e.g. olive, canola, sunflower oils.

*This table summarises the core foods and recommended serving sizes (or units) used as the basis for the recipes in this book.

DISCRETIONARY FOODS

Let's call them 'sometimes' foods and drinks! High in added sugar, salt, saturated fat and alcohol, these foods are typically low in beneficial nutrients, are often highly processed and can contribute to an energy intake that is greater than our body needs. This category includes cakes, biscuits, muffins, slices, sweets, chocolates, chips, pastries, ice cream, crackers, many cooking sauces, spreads, ready-to-eat foods, soft drinks and alcohol, and much more.

Many processed foods and drinks are an enticing combination of sweet, salty and/or rich flavours, making them hard to resist. The amount of discretionary foods we consume can creep up, especially given their convenience, marketing and availability. In fact, about one-third of the average Australian's intake of food and drinks is made up of items that fit into this category.

Half of the discretionary foods consumed by Australian adults are eaten in between main meals. If you think you could make some improvements, try replacing discretionary snack foods with other core foods of similar taste and convenience. Use snack times as an opportunity to boost your intake of nutrient-packed foods that you might not eat at your main meals, such as yoghurt, fruit and nuts, or dial up your vegetable intake with a few raw veggies. If you would like to improve your snacking and mealtime routines, try using the strategies for disrupting an unhealthy habit on page 57. With some effort, planning and adjustment, you are likely to find a few ways to cut back.

The goal does not need to be to completely eliminate discretionary foods. Rather, you may need to manage how much and how often you eat them. The Weekend Dessert recipes in this book include some indulgences as part of a healthy overall intake.

TAKE ACTION

Take some time to reflect on how often and in what quantity you consume these foods.

▸ Is it every day, or multiple times a day?

▸ Consider the circumstances. Are there particular triggers?

▸ Are there more nutritious foods or drinks you could choose instead?

▸ Have these foods become a habit? Use the strategies on page 57 to build healthier habits.

▸ Explore the healthy indulgences on pages 154–165 and 218–227.

▸ Check out the healthier alternatives to fast foods on page 85.

Sugar alternatives

While there is no evidence to suggest artificial sweeteners are not safe to consume, there is also a lack of evidence that having them instead of sugar will assist with weight loss or blood sugar control. Many food labels now promote sugar alternatives as 'derived from plants' or 'natural'. This does not necessarily make these sweeteners any more effective at controlling blood sugar levels or helping with weight loss. If you have a tendency towards being a 'sweet tooth', this can make it harder to stop eating sugary foods and drinks. Eating more core foods and fewer highly sweetened foods and drinks might help your taste preferences adjust.

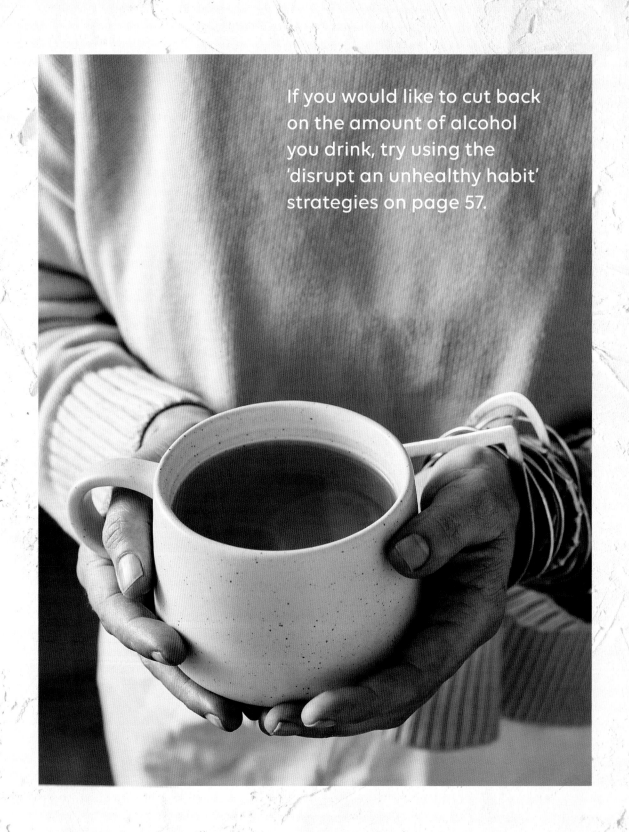

If you would like to cut back on the amount of alcohol you drink, try using the 'disrupt an unhealthy habit' strategies on page 57.

DRINKS

Tap water is the ideal choice. It contains fluoride in most parts of Australia and it's virtually free. Using a refillable water bottle is great for your health and your sustainability credentials. If you need to buy water, choose sugar-free options such as plain still, plain sparkling or soda water.

Alcohol

The evidence is clear: alcohol is bad for our health. It is linked to certain cancers and other lifestyle-related diseases. Alcoholic drinks can also contribute to weight gain because of the energy in the drinks and the food choices that often occur while you are drinking – and perhaps the next day!

Alcohol interrupts sleep rhythms and blocks Rapid Eye Movement (REM) sleep, considered to be the most restorative type of sleep. Poor sleep quality can make you feel tired and also have an impact on your eating and exercise habits.

What about soft drinks?

Sugary soft drinks, energy/sports drinks, cordials, fruit drinks, flavoured mineral waters and vitamin-style waters all have a lot of sugar and no 'nutritional value'. In fact, one 600 ml bottle of soft drink contains around 16 teaspoons of sugar. Switching to tap water will have nutritional, dental and financial benefits.

The latest Australian recommendations are to have no more than 10 standard drinks per week and no more than 4 standard drinks on any one day. There are no longer different recommendations for men and women. Many drink servings contain more than 1 standard drink. Check the label on the bottle or container.

The less you choose to drink alcohol, the lower your risk of alcohol-related harm. If you choose to drink, limit your intake. For some people, not drinking at all is the safest option. Here are some tips for cutting back on your alcohol intake:

- Turn your wine into a 'spritz' by adding mineral or soda water.
- Have a glass (or jug) of water close by to encourage alternating alcohol with water.
- There are many low-alcohol or light beer, cider and wine options available.
- Commit to designated alcohol-free days – it will soon become a habit.
- Give yourself a time or quantity limit for your final alcoholic beverage, and choose water or tea at the end of the night.

A STANDARD DRINK CONTAINS 10 G ALCOHOL

100 ML
WINE

285 ML
FULL-STRENGTH
BEER

30 ML
SPIRIT

Make it real

As we have mentioned throughout this book, our goal is to move women towards making lifelong healthy food and activity choices, and away from a 'restrictive' approach.

One way to use this book is to simply start incorporating the recipes into your everyday cooking repertoire. Another way is to use the sample meal plan on pages 80–81 and the food unit breakdown in the recipes to become more familiar with putting together a day's meals.

The recipes for the main meals in this book have been designed to provide 4 servings. This is a guide for quantities only. If you are physically active or a bigger person, these meals are unlikely to be enough food for you and may result in gradual weight loss. If weight loss is something that you are aiming for and you want a more structured weight loss approach, the CSIRO has other publications and programs to suit those needs, such as *The CSIRO Total Wellbeing Diet* and *The CSIRO Low-Carb Diet*.

The food unit breakdown in the recipes is consistent with previous CSIRO books, making it easy to incorporate them into other CSIRO structured eating programs. For a more personalised approach to changing the way you eat, we also recommend consulting an Accredited Practising Dietitian.

HALF OF
YOUR PLATE:
VEGETABLES

ONE QUARTER OF
YOUR PLATE: MEAT/
ALTERNATIVES

ONE QUARTER OF
YOUR PLATE: GRAINS
OR STARCHY VEG

SAMPLE MEAL PLAN

1
Breakfast
Wholegrain, dairy, fruit, healthy oil (nuts/seeds)

2
Morning tea
Dairy

3
Lunch
Wholegrain, vegetables, healthy oil, meat/alternatives

MILKY COFFEE

OAT AND APPLE BOWL, PAGE 93

STACK AND PACK CREAMY EGG AND RICE SALAD JAR, PAGE 100

WEEKEND OPTIONS

▶ Have a protein-rich breakfast.

▶ Share a healthy platter with friends – ideas on pages 194–195.

SALMON AND MASH SIMPLE SPICE-BOOSTER BOWL, PAGE 127

4
Afternoon tea
Fruit

5
Dinner
Wholegrains, vegetables, healthy oil, meat/alternatives

6
Healthy dessert
Dairy, fruit, healthy oil (nuts/seeds)

PASSIONFRUIT CHIA YOGHURT 'JELLIES', PAGE 159

TIPS FOR BIGGER APPETITES

▸ There is always room for more vegetables. Add a salad to the meal for everyone to help themselves.

▸ Add extra grains, such as pasta, rice, quinoa or couscous, or starchy vegetables, such as potatoes or sweet potatoes.

MAKING MEALS WORK FOR EVERYONE

While this section is aimed at families with children at home, the same principles apply to catering for groups of people with different tastes. Every home and every family is unique; therefore, mealtime routines will be too.

It's worth taking stock of your household's meal habits to consider whether there are any areas that could be changed for the better:

- Do you run out the door without breakfast, then find yourself looking for a mid-morning snack that perhaps isn't the best choice?
- Is your household sitting down together for dinner as often as you would like?
- Do you intend to take lunch to work but usually find yourself buying it, or working through lunch and skipping it all together?

A routine of three main meals might not always be easy but the benefits include:

- more even portion control across the day;
- less potential for overeating at subsequent meals;
- more opportunities for consuming foods from the core food groups;
- more opportunities to connect as a family and for you to model healthy eating habits.

A small snack in between meals can be part of a balanced eating pattern, but often 'snacking' can lead to 'grazing' on discretionary foods.

Batch cooking

Batch cooking will save you time and money and reduce the odds of ending up with a takeaway. Once you are enjoying some weeknights without having to cook, you'll be hooked. Here are some tips to make it work for you:

- Be prepared. Make sure you have time to complete a large cook and are reducing your stress rather than adding to it.
- Make sure you have plenty of containers in the sizes you need.
- Label the containers. Include a 'best before' date. The food you plan to eat in the next few days can be stored in the fridge; the rest needs to be frozen.
- Plan your menu. Consider which meals will double as a different dish. A bolognese sauce can be used for spaghetti or jacket potatoes, or transformed into a chilli con carne with added black beans and our Mexican spice booster (see page 122).
- Buy key ingredients in bulk, such as rice, pasta, dried legumes, nuts and seeds.
- Use time-saving devices such as food processors, slow cookers, pressure cookers, box graters, kitchen scissors and a mandolin.
- The cooking time will be longer for double batches. Use the original cooking time as a guide, then monitor your dish for doneness.
- Undercook your veggies slightly, as they will continue cooking when you reheat them later.
- Take care with food hygiene. Make sure you fully cool food before freezing.

Family-friendly ideas

No-one needs the hassle of making separate meals for each member of the household. The following meal topper ideas will help all diners to enjoy a single meal. The toppers can be offered at the table, or mixed in prior to serving.

ADDITIONS FOR ADVENTUROUS TASTEBUDS

Chilli flakes, powder, sauce, jam or sriracha

Spices, such as sumac, paprika or cumin, or spice mixes such as dukkah

Pepper

Sautéed garlic and onion

Relish

Acid, such as vinegar or lemon juice or zest

Fresh herbs, such as coriander, dill, basil, parsley, rosemary, oregano

Mustard

Toasted nuts

Chopped olives, capers or pickles

Greek yoghurt mixed with fresh herbs and a squeeze of lemon juice

ADDITIONS FOR TIMID TASTEBUDS

Dash of milk or yoghurt to dilute strong flavours

Low-salt stock

Low-salt soy sauce

Grated cheese

All-purpose seasoning instead of spice

Low-salt tomato sauce or mayonnaise

Low-salt American (yellow) mustard

Dollop of natural yoghurt

Food storage tips

+ Transfer leftovers into airtight containers and store them in the fridge or freezer.
+ Meals with cooked carbs can be stored in the fridge for no more than 3 days, or frozen. You can defrost your meal in the fridge before reheating on a stove top or in the microwave straight from frozen. Make sure it's piping hot before eating and don't reheat more than once.
+ Fresh chillies and ginger can be stored in the freezer for up to 6 months. Just slice or grate off as needed.
+ Keep your soft herbs, such as coriander, parsley and mint, fresh longer by washing in cold water, then draining (or spinning in a salad spinner), loosely wrapping them in damp paper towel and placing them in the fridge crisper.

THE SUSTAINABLE KITCHEN

Currently, the food system is estimated to contribute to over a quarter of global greenhouse emissions. There is plenty we, as food consumers, can do to limit our contribution to this effect.

Cut back on junk food

The greenhouse gas emissions associated with the types and amounts of foods that the average Australian adult consumes have been analysed. Discretionary foods (see page 75) contributed almost one-third (29 per cent) to total food-related greenhouse gas emissions. So purchasing fewer discretionary foods and drinks can make a difference to both sustainability measures and our health.

Fresh meat also contributes approximately a third of food-related greenhouse gas emissions, but this food group is packed with high-quality protein and nutrients that are important for health. Including some meat-free meals can help improve personal sustainability. Try the vegetarian meals in this book.

Eat seasonally

There are many benefits to eating produce that is in season – it is generally cheaper, tastier and sourced locally. However, global distribution, better storage systems and processing methods have ensured that many foods are now available year-round. While it is great to be able to access extra variety throughout the year, this comes with a level of disconnection from the natural world and understanding of seasonal differences.

The recipes in this book have been designed to be able to swap and substitute ingredients to make the most of seasonal availability and minimise waste.

Reduce food waste

Approximately 30–50 per cent of all food produced is not eaten, but goes to waste. This loss occurs at every step – from production, processing, distribution and retail through to household consumption.

Here are some ways you can reduce your personal food waste:

- Plan your meals for the coming week, write a shopping list and only buy what you need. You'll have fewer trips to the shops, the right ingredients on hand for nutritious meals and you'll avoid unused, spoiled produce.

- When buying seasonal produce, stick to a few varieties and use them in multiple recipes. This works well for items like cauliflower, pumpkin, herbs, carrots and potatoes.

- Make an 'end-of-week' soup, slow cook or combo salad to use up remaining veggies.

- Use a compost bucket or pick up a kitchen caddy and compostable bags from your local council for your food scraps if they have a green organics bin scheme. This reduces waste going to landfill, increases resource recovery and reduces greenhouse emissions.

- Put leftovers into airtight containers and store them in the fridge or freezer according to when you plan to eat them.

BEATING TAKEAWAY

These homemade meal ideas are cheaper, healthier and tastier.

- ▶ PIZZA. Add extra veggies such as mushrooms, zucchini, fresh tomato, red onion, capsicum, eggplant, pumpkin, squash or broccoli before cooking, and fresh baby spinach or rocket after cooking.
- ▶ OVEN-BAKED CHIPS. Make your own (even easier to leave the skin on!) or choose the frozen oven-baked options that use healthy unsaturated oils and don't have added salt. Look for the varieties with the highest Health Star Rating. Airfryers can be used to get the same crunch without the oil, for either homemade or store-bought chips.
- ▶ BURGERS. Try the Turkey breast burger on page 106, or the Horseradish steak sandwich on page 186 for a healthy alternative.
- ▶ CRISPY FISH AND CHIPS. Crumb your fish in wholemeal breadcrumbs or panko for a crispy texture and bake in the oven or shallow-fry in unsaturated oil.
- ▶ BURRITOS/TACOS. Try the Mexi-bowl recipe on page 126.

TIPS FOR EATING OUT

- ▶ INDIAN: Choose a mixed vegetable curry (jalfrezi) or saag paneer, which is blended spinach with cheese. Try the lentil dish, dahl, as a side. Avoid the deep-fried offerings, such as pakoras.
- ▶ ASIAN: There are usually plenty of vegetarian options at Asian restaurants so take the opportunity to boost your veggie intake. A san choy bau (lettuce cups with chicken and veggies) is a good choice or a Thai larb, which is chicken mince with herbs.
- ▶ MEXICAN: There are plenty of good options here if you ask them to go heavy on the salad and avoid excessive sauces and corn chips.

- ● Find ways to pack in extra vegetables. Ask for a side salad or bowl of steamed vegetables. Consider getting it before the main meal so you can munch on the veggies rather than bread or other nibbles.
- ● Ask for double or even triple the vegetables.
- ● Ask for sauces and dressings on the side so you can decide how much to have.
- ● Avoid the temptation of upsizing and 'meal deals'.
- ● Choose water as your beverage.
- ● Don't be too shy to ask for a meal the way you want it: side salad instead of a bread bowl, veggies instead of fries, water instead of soft drink.
- ● Choose grilled instead of fried.

FAQ

Our food-loving dietitians answer your common questions

Q The 'protein' and 'grains/starchy foods' (like potatoes) always seem to make up more than half of my plate. How do I cut back?

A Make sure your veggies take up half the plate. Spend effort adding flavour with spice boosters, nuts, garlic and low-salt sauces. And be careful not to overcook them. Check out page 65 for tips on increasing your vegetable intake. All the recipes in this book have plenty of veggies.

Q I have lunch (usually a Vegemite sandwich and a banana) but I still get drowsy and crave sweets in the afternoon. What's going on?

A Try to add a protein source at lunchtime to help you feel fuller for longer. Great examples include: lean meat, such as chicken or turkey, fish, such as tuna or salmon, dairy, such as cheese or a tub of yoghurt, eggs and legumes, such as hummus. This is also the case at breakfast, so make sure you include protein in your morning meal as well. Try the protein-rich breakfast recipes in this book. In addition, try going for a walk outside in the afternoon, rather than snacking.

Q By the time my kids (and me, if I'm being honest) have snacked their way through the afternoon, they don't feel hungry for their evening meal. How do I manage that after-school period?

A Prepare a selection of healthy snacks and have them ready to grab. Some cut-up raw vegetables can be really successful here. When they are finished, no more snacks until the evening meal. Check that you, and your kids, are feeling actual hunger and not eating out of habit, boredom, fatigue or stress. It can also help to manage the kids' hunger by eating dinner earlier during the school term. Finally, check that breakfast and lunch are filling and include some healthy protein.

Q I'm too busy to make home-cooked meals. How do I fit in all the cooking?

A Set aside some time on weekends for preparing make-ahead meals (see pages 96–103 and 208–211). Select meals that are simple and quick to prepare during the week – there are plenty of 'almost instant' recipes in this book. Invent your own 'tray-baked complete meal' combination that can cook away while you get a few other jobs done. You could share the load by involving your partner and any older children in planning and preparing meals.

It also comes down to prioritising this important activity. Meal prep and eating together as a family can easily be hijacked by extracurricular and other commitments, so be easy on yourself and gradually make new healthy habits. See pages 56–57 for ways to form healthy habits.

Q My kids always whine about their evening meal. How do I get them interested in eating healthy meals?

A Try involving the kids in the meal preparation, from planning the meals, to shopping and then cooking. The weekends are a good time to introduce kids to cooking and as they get older, you may even be able to allocate a regular weekday for them to prepare a meal. It gives them experience and responsibility and takes the pressure off you! Also check out the tips for making one meal work for everyone on page 82.

Q I know physical activity is important but whenever I start exercising more I get really hungry and I tend to overeat. What can I do to control my appetite?

A There are plenty of ways to refuel without overdoing it. Try to avoid getting too hungry. This could mean having a snack, such as a piece of fruit, trail mix or nut butter on crispbread, soon after exercise. Alternatively, try scheduling exercise just before a main meal. Rehydrate to quench your thirst and ensure you're not confusing thirst with hunger. Foods that contain protein help manage appetite, so try to include protein in most meals (see page 68 for more info).

PART THREE

the recipes

NOURISHING YOU

week

days

BERRYLICIOUS BOWL

MONKEY BIZ BOWL

OAT AND APPLE BOWL

Fast breakfast bowls

These breakfast bowls are designed for mornings when time is tight. Simply layer the ingredients in your bowl in whatever order you like for a simple, nutrient-packed start to your day. The type of cereal can be changed to suit your personal preference and, of course, you can mix and match the optional extras depending on what's in your pantry.

EACH BREAKFAST BOWL SERVES 1

Berrylicious bowl

200 g vanilla yoghurt
60 g wheat cereal flakes
150 g mixed frozen
    berries, thawed
2 teaspoons toasted
    walnuts, crushed

Optional extra

1 teaspoon pure maple syrup
    (or honey)

Monkey biz bowl

250 ml (1 cup) milk
60 g Sultana Bran®
1 medium banana, sliced
2 teaspoons toasted
    flaked almonds

Optional extra

1 teaspoon desiccated coconut

UNITS PER SERVE • GRAIN 2 • DAIRY 1 • OIL 1 • FRUIT 1

TROPICAL
DREAM BOWL

TIP
Choose a variety
of fruit that is at its
seasonal best.

STICKY DATE
BRAN BOWL

Oat and apple bowl

200 g natural Greek-style
   yoghurt
60 g instant oats
1 medium red apple, cut
   into matchsticks
2 teaspoons pumpkin
   seeds (pepitas)

Optional extra
¼ teaspoon ground cinnamon

Tropical dream bowl

200 g mango yoghurt
60 g natural muesli
1 medium banana, halved
2 teaspoons toasted Brazil nuts,
   finely chopped

Optional extra
¼ teaspoon ground ginger

Sticky date bran bowl

200 g natural Greek-style
   yoghurt
60 g All-Bran flakes®
30 g pitted medjool dates (about
   1½ dates), finely chopped
2 teaspoons walnuts, crushed

Optional extra
¼ teaspoon mixed spice

JUST PEACHY

CHOC-BANANA

Breakfast smoothies

These smoothie recipes are good for those of us who prefer a lighter meal in the morning. You might find it handy to keep a stash of peeled, roughly chopped ripe bananas in a zip-lock bag or container in the freezer, ready to go. Simply place all the ingredients in an upright blender (or use a stick blender) and blitz until smooth. Serve immediately.

EACH SMOOTHIE SERVES 1

Choc-banana

250 ml (1 cup) milk of choice
2 teaspoons cocoa powder
1 medium over-ripe
   banana, frozen
2 teaspoons toasted
   flaked almonds

Optional topping
extra pinch cocoa powder

Just peachy

250 ml (1 cup) milk of choice
2 teaspoons toasted walnuts
¼ teaspoon freshly grated
   (or ground) nutmeg
150 g drained tinned peaches

Optional topping
freshly grated nutmeg

UNITS PER SERVE • DAIRY 1 • OIL 1 • FRUIT 1

FRESH BERRY

LEMON AND BLUEBERRY CHEESECAKE

TIP

Add a handful of ice cubes prior to blitzing. This will give your smoothie more of a 'thickshake' consistency and is refreshing during the warmer months.

BASIC SMOOTHIE

Fresh berry

125 ml (½ cup) milk of choice
100 g natural Greek-style
    yoghurt
2 teaspoons avocado
½ teaspoon ground ginger
a few mint leaves
150 g frozen berries

Optional topping
mint leaves

Basic smoothie

125 ml (½ cup) milk of choice
100 g yoghurt of choice
1 teaspoon vanilla extract
1 medium over-ripe
    banana, frozen
1 teaspoon peanut (or other nut)
    butter
1 tablespoon bran (oat or wheat)

Lemon and blueberry cheesecake

125 ml (½ cup) milk of choice
100 g lemon yoghurt
1 teaspoon tahini
1 tablespoon lemon juice
150 g frozen blueberries

Optional topping
pinch finely grated lemon zest

Prep your weekday grains

A great tip to make your weekday meals quick and easy to prepare is to pre-cook batches of grains, such as rice, quinoa and pasta. Then simply reheat them when needed. Any leftovers can be frozen into portion sizes to use at a later date, noting that the longer they're frozen, the more their texture will be affected. For details on how to safely cook, freeze then reheat your grains see the 'Food storage tips' section on page 83.

The recipes in this book allow for 1 cup cooked grains per serve (and four serves per recipe). You may want to alter the quantity of grains to suit your needs, using the following conversions as a quick guide for cooking.

QUICK CONVERSION GUIDE FOR COOKING GRAINS

½ cup (about 50 g) uncooked pasta/noodles	1 cup cooked pasta/noodles
⅓ cup (about 70 g) uncooked rice	1 cup cooked rice
⅓ cup (about 60 g) uncooked quinoa/freekeh	1 cup cooked quinoa/freekeh
¼ cup (about 50 g) uncooked pearl barley/buckwheat	1 cup cooked pearl barley/buckwheat

Buckwheat

Cook the buckwheat in a saucepan of boiling water for 25–30 minutes or until tender. Drain and refresh under cold running water, then transfer to a large bowl and set aside.

Noodles

Noodles generally just need to be soaked before use. Follow the directions on the packet – some require water that has just come to the boil, others simply use cold water.

Pasta

Bring the water to full boil (allow approximately 1 litre of water for each 100 g of dry pasta to be cooked). Add the pasta and then cook until al dente. The cooking time depends on the shape of the pasta so follow the instructions on the packet. Drain and refresh under cold running water, then transfer to a large bowl and set aside.

TIP

Meals with cooked grains can be stored in the fridge for up to 3 days or in the freezer.

NOODLES

BUCKWHEAT

PASTA

PEARL BARLEY

RICE

QUINOA

FREEKEH

Quinoa

Rinse the quinoa, then cook in a saucepan of boiling water for 12–15 minutes or until tender. You will know it is ready when the quinoa kernels look like they have 'popped open'. Drain and refresh under cold running water, then transfer to a large bowl and set aside.

Pearl barley

Cook the pearl barley in a large saucepan of boiling water for 35–40 minutes or until tender. Pearl barley should triple in size when it is cooked. Drain and refresh under cold running water, then transfer to a large bowl and set aside.

Freekeh

Bring a saucepan of water to the boil over high heat, add the freekeh and cook for 25–35 minutes or until the freekeh looks swollen and soft. Drain and refresh under cold running water. Drain again.

Rice

Measure the amount of rice you need. For long-grain rice, it is important to rinse before cooking to remove any excess starch. You can do this by placing the rice in a sieve and rinsing thoroughly in cold water until the water runs clear. For white rice, add double the amount of water (2 cups, or 500 ml, water for each 1 cup of rice); you'll need a bit more water for brown rice. Bring the water to the boil over high heat, add the rice, set the heat to very low, cover the saucepan with a lid and cook until just tender. The cooking time will vary, depending on the type of rice you use. As a rough guide, brown basmati rice takes 12–15 minutes, white rice takes 15–18 minutes, and regular brown rice takes 25–35 minutes, but check the packet instructions if you're unsure. You can also microwave rice in a microwave rice cooker – add double the water to rice and microwave on high for 15 minutes. There might be slight variations, depending on the rice and the microwave, but once you get to know your microwave you will cook perfect fluffy rice every time!

Stack-and-pack portable lunches

These make a perfectly portable meal that can be eaten straight from the container or tipped into a bowl to serve. Simply stack the ingredients, in the order shown, into a screw-top glass jar or container. You can make a few at once so that you're organised for the days ahead. If you find these aren't quite satisfying enough, add extra salad vegetables, or increase the amount of grain/carbohydrate.

EACH SALAD SERVES 1

Creamy egg and rice

¼ x quantity Garlic citrus yoghurt 3-in-1 (page 138)
80 g (½ cup) cooked brown basmati rice (see page 99)
2 large hard-boiled eggs, peeled and chopped
1 small carrot, coarsely grated
1 stick celery, thinly sliced
½ cup baby spinach leaves
1 tablespoon toasted slivered almonds

Italian salmon pasta

¼ x quantity Italian balsamic 3-in-1 (page 138)
80 g (½ cup) cooked wholegrain pasta, such as fusilli
100 g drained tinned salmon, crushed
40 g (½ cup) drained artichoke hearts in brine, halved
3 tablespoons corn kernels
1 tomato, chopped
20 g chopped avocado
½ cup flat-leaf parsley leaves

Dairy option
40 g shaved parmesan

CREAMY EGG AND RICE

ITALIAN SALMON PASTA

Soy-sesame chicken and noodles

¼ x quantity Soy, sesame and ginger 3-in-1 (page 138)
80 g (½ cup) soaked brown rice vermicelli noodles
100 g sliced cooked chicken
½ red capsicum, seeded and thinly sliced
60 g (½ cup) frozen baby peas
1 spring onion, thinly sliced
2 teaspoons toasted unsalted cashews, finely chopped

Tahini tofu and sweet potato

½ x quantity Tahini and lime 3-in-1 (page 139)
170 g firm tofu, chopped
(or ½ x 400 g tin chickpeas, drained and rinsed)
125 g cherry tomatoes, halved
150 g chopped roast sweet potato
4 baby cos leaves, shredded
2 tablespoons chopped chives

Mustard tuna and pasta

¼ x quantity Mustard and lemon 3-in-1 (page 139)
80 g (½ cup) cooked pasta, such as risoni
100 g drained tinned tuna in springwater
1 small Lebanese cucumber, finely chopped
1 cup baby rocket leaves
2 tablespoons chopped basil
2 teaspoons toasted walnuts, chopped

Dairy option
40 g Greek feta, crumbled

UNITS PER SERVE • MEAT & ALT 1 • GRAIN 1 • VEGETABLES 2 • OIL 2

TAHINI TOFU AND SWEET POTATO

SOY-SESAME CHICKEN AND NOODLES

MUSTARD TUNA AND PASTA

JAPANESE TOFU

SPRING CHICKEN

CHICKEN KORMA

Freezer-friendly batch soups

To make the soup, start by preparing the grain, if it's not already cooked. Then heat the oil or paste in a large saucepan over medium heat. Add the protein and cook, stirring, for 2–3 minutes until well coated and starting to turn light golden. Add the vegetables and other ingredients. Simmer, partially covered, for 20–30 minutes or until the protein is cooked. Cool slightly. Divide the grain among portion-sized freezer-safe containers, then add the soup. Cover and freeze. Thaw in the fridge and gently reheat on the stovetop or in the microwave on medium. Make sure the soup is piping hot before eating. Add the optional topping, if using, and serve.

EACH SOUP BATCH SERVES 4

Japanese tofu

360 g (2 cups) cooked
   buckwheat (page 96)
1 tablespoon sunflower oil
1 teaspoon sesame oil
700 g firm tofu, chopped
2 baby bok choy, leaves separated
500 g peeled, chopped pumpkin
300 g baby green beans, halved
1.5 litres salt-reduced
   vegetable stock
2 tablespoons salt-reduced
   soy sauce
3 cm piece ginger, grated

Optional topping
sliced spring onion

Chicken korma

320 g (2 cups) cooked brown
   basmati rice (page 99)
1 tablespoon korma curry paste
400 g diced chicken breast
1 onion, chopped
2 carrots, chopped
1 large red capsicum, seeded
   and chopped
1.5 litres salt-reduced chicken
   stock

Optional topping
coriander leaves

FISH LAKSA

ITALIAN BEEF

TIP
Adapt these recipes to use up any ingredients that have been sitting in your fridge a little too long. You can also double the quantities and freeze some for later.

Spring chicken

360 g (2 cups) cooked
    quinoa (page 99)
2 tablespoons olive oil
400 g chicken stir-fry strips
1 bunch asparagus, chopped
2 zucchini, chopped
2 cups baby spinach leaves
1.5 litres salt-reduced
    chicken stock
2 cloves garlic, crushed

Optional topping
chopped chives

Italian beef

320 g (2 cups) cooked
    wholegrain fusilli
2 tablespoons olive oil
400 g diced beef
1 red onion, chopped
6 yellow squash, sliced
2 bulbs baby fennel or
    ½ bulb fennel, finely chopped
1 litre salt-reduced beef stock
400 g tin crushed tomatoes

Optional topping
basil leaves

Fish laksa

320 g (2 cups) soaked brown rice
    vermicelli noodles
1 tablespoon red curry paste
400 g skinless, boneless thick
    white fish fillet, chopped
300 g snow peas, trimmed
1 green capsicum, seeded
    and sliced
300 g fresh baby corn,
    halved lengthways
1.5 litres salt-reduced
    chicken stock

Optional topping
mint leaves
lime juice

UNITS PER SERVE • MEAT & ALT 1 • GRAIN 1 • VEGETABLES 2 • OIL 1–2

weekday dinner

Turkey breast burger with pumpkin fries

SERVES **4**
PREPARATION **20 MINUTES**
COOKING **25 MINUTES**

Chicken breast can be used in place of the turkey breast steaks, if preferred. To speed up the cooking time, you can tenderise the meat by pounding it with a mallet (or a rolling pin) to make it a little thinner.

---

1 kg peeled pumpkin, cut into 1 cm-thick fries
olive oil cooking spray
600 g turkey breast steaks, seasoned with freshly ground black pepper
1 red onion, very thinly sliced into rounds
½ x quantity Mustard and lemon 3-in-1 (see page 139)
4 x 80 g multigrain rolls, split
2 tablespoons hummus
2 Lebanese cucumbers, peeled into long thin strips
2 cups mixed salad leaves

Preheat the oven to 220°C (200°C fan-forced). Line a large baking tray with baking paper.

Add the pumpkin to the prepared tray, spray lightly with oil and season with freshly ground black pepper. Roast for 10 minutes, then turn the fries over. Add the turkey to the tray alongside the fries, spray with oil and roast for another 15 minutes or until cooked and golden.

Meanwhile, combine the onion and 3-in-1 in a bowl. Set aside, tossing occasionally until the onion softens.

Place the rolls on serving plates and spread with hummus. Top with the turkey, then the onion mixture, cucumber and salad leaves. Serve with the pumpkin fries.

UNITS PER SERVE • MEAT & ALT 1.5 • GRAIN 2 • VEGETABLES 3 • OIL 2

Chicken and vegetable penne

SERVES **4**
PREPARATION **15 MINUTES**
COOKING **20 MINUTES**

Do your kids struggle with onion? Try using golden shallots, as they are a little sweeter with a less astringent flavour. Another tip to soften the flavour of onion is to soak it in cold water before adding it to a dish. Serve the pasta with grated parmesan for an optional boost of flavour, or a sprinkling of chilli if you like a bit of heat.

---

2 tablespoons extra virgin
   olive oil
600 g diced chicken breast
1 onion, thinly sliced
2 cloves garlic, crushed
2 zucchini, cut into thick
   matchsticks
70 g (½ cup) drained sundried
   tomato in brine, cut into strips
240 g (2 cups) frozen peas
1 cup basil leaves, torn
finely grated zest and juice of
   1 small lemon
640 g (4 cups) cooked
   wholegrain penne

Heat the oil in a large, deep non-stick frying pan over medium–high heat. Add the chicken and cook, stirring occasionally, for 5 minutes.

Reduce the heat to medium. Add the onion, garlic and zucchini and cook, stirring occasionally, for 10 minutes. Stir in the sundried tomato and peas and cook for 1 minute.

Add the remaining ingredients and cook, tossing, for 1–2 minutes or until heated through and well combined. Season with freshly ground black pepper and serve.

UNITS PER SERVE • MEAT & ALT 1.5 • GRAIN 2 • VEGETABLES 3 • OIL 2

Chargrilled Mexican chicken salad

SERVES **4**
PREPARATION **20 MINUTES**
COOKING **15 MINUTES**

Sometimes 'bowl food' is just what is called for at the end of a busy day – comforting and easy to eat. Try cutting your pita bread into wedges, then bake them in the oven for a few minutes to make 'crisps'. This dish is even more delicious topped with a dollop of natural yoghurt.

600 g chicken breast stir-fry strips
1 tablespoon Mexican spice booster (see page 122)
500 g peeled pumpkin, thinly sliced
1 tablespoon olive oil
2 Lebanese cucumbers, chopped
250 g cherry tomatoes, halved
1 cup mint leaves
4 cups baby spinach leaves
1 x quantity Mustard and lemon 3-in-1 (see page 139)
4 x 80 g wholemeal pita breads

Heat a large chargrill plate (or large frying pan if you don't have a grill plate) over high heat.

Combine the chicken, spice booster, pumpkin and oil in a large bowl, tossing to coat evenly.

Working in three batches, chargrill the chicken mixture for 4–5 minutes each. Transfer to a large serving bowl.

Add the cucumber, tomato, mint, spinach and Mustard and lemon 3-in-1 to the chicken mixture and gently toss to combine. Season with freshly ground black pepper and serve warm with pita breads.

UNITS PER SERVE • MEAT & ALT 1.5 • GRAIN 2 • VEGETABLES 3+ • OIL 2

Family tray bake

WEEKDAY DINNER

SERVES 4
PREPARATION 20 MINUTES
COOKING 25 MINUTES

For family members with a more developed palate, offer a few extra ingredients: pitted olives, basil leaves, drained capers, or chilli. Serve them in small bowls at the table.

CHILD

2 tablespoons extra virgin olive oil
1 tablespoon All-purpose spice booster (see page 122)
600 g washed baby potatoes, halved
600 g chicken tenderloins
2 red onions, peeled and cut into wedges
1 head broccoli, florets separated, stems thickly sliced
800 g baby tomato medley mix
2 cups baby rocket leaves
lemon wedges, to serve (optional)

Preheat the oven to 200°C (180°C fan-forced). Line a large baking tray with baking paper.

Combine the oil, spice booster, potatoes, chicken, onion, broccoli and tomatoes in a large bowl. Season with freshly ground black pepper and toss well to coat, then spread the mixture evenly over the prepared tray.

Bake for 20–25 minutes or until cooked and golden. Scatter over the rocket and serve with lemon wedges alongside (if using).

UNITS PER SERVE
• MEAT & ALT 1.5
• GRAIN 2
• VEGETABLES 3+
• OIL 2

TEENAGER

ADULT

TODDLER

Mild turkey curry

SERVES **4**
PREPARATION **15 MINUTES**
COOKING **20 MINUTES**

Chicken breast fillets can be used in place of the turkey if that's what you happen to have. Naan bread can be bought fresh from most supermarkets. If you are feeling adventurous, try making your own – kneading dough is a sure-fire way to get kids into the kitchen.

1 tablespoon sunflower oil
3 teaspoons Indian spice booster
   (see page 121)
600 g turkey breast, chopped
2 large carrots, chopped
2 zucchini, chopped
2 x 400 g tins crushed tomatoes
1 head broccoli, florets
   separated, stems chopped
1 tablespoon toasted unsalted
   cashews (optional)
½ cup coriander leaves
4 x 80 g wholemeal naan breads,
   warmed

Heat the oil in a large saucepan over medium–high heat. Add the spice booster and turkey and cook, stirring occasionally, for 5 minutes. Add the carrot, zucchini, tomatoes and 500 ml (2 cups) water. Bring to the boil.

Reduce the heat to medium and simmer, stirring occasionally, for 5 minutes. Add the broccoli and simmer, stirring occasionally, for 5 minutes more or until the vegetables are tender and the liquid has reduced by half. Season with freshly ground black pepper.

Divide the curry among serving bowls. Top with the cashews, if using, and coriander and serve with naan bread alongside.

UNITS PER SERVE • MFAT & ALT 1.5 • GRAIN 2 • VEGETABLES 4 • OIL 2

Chicken stir-fry

SERVES **4**
PREPARATION **15 MINUTES**
COOKING **10 MINUTES**

You can marinate the chicken in the 3-in-1 for up to 2 days and keep it covered in the fridge until you're ready to cook. This is a great opportunity to ask your children to help prepare the vegetables, as there is no need for the chopping to be very precise. Brown rice takes a bit longer to cook, but the extra time is worth it – it provides twice as much fibre as white rice.

1 x quantity Soy, sesame and
    ginger 3-in-1 (see page 138)
600 g chicken stir-fry strips
2 bunches broccolini, trimmed
    and halved lengthways
2 carrots, cut into thick
    matchsticks
1 large red capsicum, seeded
    and thickly sliced
300 g sugar snap peas, trimmed
2 spring onions, cut into 2 cm
    lengths
640 g (4 cups) cooked brown rice
    (see page 99)
1 ½ tablespoons toasted
    unsalted peanuts, chopped

Combine the 3-in-1 and chicken in a bowl and set aside (if you can, leave it to marinate while you're prepping the rice and vegetables).

Heat a large non-stick wok over high heat. Cook the chicken in three batches, stir-frying each batch for 2 minutes. Transfer to a bowl.

Add the broccolini, carrot, capsicum and sugar snaps to the wok and stir-fry for 2–3 minutes or until starting to soften. Return the chicken to the wok, add the spring onion and stir-fry for 1 minute.

Spoon the rice into bowls, add the chicken stir-fry and sprinkle with peanuts to serve.

UNITS PER SERVE • MEAT & ALT **1.5** • GRAIN **2** • VEGETABLES **3** • OIL **2**

THIS IS A GOOD RECIPE FOR CHILDREN WHO PREFER EACH MEAL COMPONENT TO BE KEPT SEPARATE ON THEIR PLATE, RATHER THAN MIXED TOGETHER.

Thai salmon and rice noodle salad

SERVES **4**
PREPARATION **20 MINUTES**
COOKING **15 MINUTES**

You can try other varieties of fish in this recipe, such as Australian mackerel, pink snapper or flathead. Similarly, regular cabbage or lettuce can be used in place of Chinese cabbage. Enjoy heat in your Thai meals? Add some chilli powder to the Soy, sesame and ginger 3-in-1.

1 tablespoon Asian spice booster (see page 122)

4 x 150 g skinless, boneless salmon fillets, cut into 2 cm pieces

1 ½ tablespoons sunflower oil

160 g (2 cups) finely shredded Chinese cabbage

250 g cherry tomatoes, halved

1 large carrot, cut into thin matchsticks

300 g snow peas, trimmed, halved lengthways

½ x quantity Soy, sesame and ginger 3-in-1 (see page 138)

640 g (4 cups) soaked brown rice vermicelli noodles

Combine the spice booster, salmon and oil in a bowl and set aside.

Place all the remaining ingredients in a large serving bowl and toss to combine (or keep separate – see tip opposite). Set aside.

Heat a large non-stick wok over high heat. Stir-fry the salmon in three batches for 3–4 minutes each or until just cooked and golden crisp. Transfer directly to the noodle mixture and gently toss through. Serve warm.

UNITS PER SERVE • **MEAT & ALT** 1.5 • **GRAIN** 2 • **VEGETABLES** 3 • **OIL** 2

Prawn and silverbeet fusilli

SERVES **4**
PREPARATION **15 MINUTES**
COOKING **10 MINUTES**

This is a great recipe for a light and fresh pasta dish. If you feel like getting creative, add some basil or dill, capers or olives, and maybe even a sprinkling of fresh chilli on top. You can use fresh spinach or a 250 g packet of frozen spinach in place of the silverbeet.

2 tablespoons olive oil
1 large red onion, cut into
   thin wedges
2 large sticks celery, thinly sliced
4 cloves garlic, crushed
600 g peeled, deveined small
   raw prawns
1 bunch silverbeet, white cores
   removed and leaves thickly
   sliced
300 g cherry tomatoes
640 g (4 cups) cooked
   wholegrain fusilli
finely grated zest and juice of
   1 large lemon

Heat the oil in a large, deep non-stick frying pan over high heat. Add the onion and celery and cook, stirring occasionally, for 3 minutes. Add the garlic and prawns and cook, tossing, for 1 minute. Add the silverbeet and toss for 1–2 minutes or until wilted.

Add the tomatoes, pasta and lemon zest and juice. Cook, tossing, for 1–2 minutes or until the prawns are cooked through and the ingredients are well combined. Season with freshly ground black pepper and serve.

UNITS PER SERVE • MEAT & ALT 1.5 • GRAIN 2 • VEGETABLES 3 • OIL 2

Tuna and quinoa toss

SERVES **4**
PREPARATION **20 MINUTES**
COOKING **10 MINUTES**

Quinoa is high in nutrients and is a great gluten-free option, but if you don't have quinoa in the cupboard use brown rice instead. It's well worth rinsing the quinoa before cooking – it removes a slight bitterness, giving a better end result.

---

4 small corn cobs, husks and silks removed

1 small head cauliflower, florets separated, stem sliced

2 spring onions, thinly sliced

600 g drained tinned tuna chunks in springwater

720 g (4 cups) cooked quinoa (see page 99)

2 cups baby rocket leaves

1 bunch radishes, thinly sliced

150 g baby cucumbers (Qukes®), very thinly sliced into rounds

1 x quantity Italian balsamic 3-in-1 (see page 138)

3 tablespoons toasted mixed seeds (pumpkin seeds/ pepitas, linseeds, sunflower seeds)

Heat a chargrill pan over high heat.

Chargrill the corn cobs and cauliflower for 8–10 minutes, turning occasionally, until cooked and golden crisp. Scoop the cauliflower into a large serving bowl. Transfer the corn to a board, then carefully cut away the kernels and add to the bowl.

Add all the remaining ingredients to the bowl and season with freshly ground black pepper. Toss together well and serve.

UNITS PER SERVE • MEAT & ALT 1.5 • GRAIN 2 • VEGETABLES 3 • OIL 2

Pork and chickpea stew

SERVES **4**
PREPARATION **20 MINUTES**
COOKING **20 MINUTES**

The kale can be replaced with other leafy greens, such as collard greens, Swiss chard or mustard greens. This stew is a great way to use up leftover veg: simply add them to the sweet potato mix with the kale and chickpeas.

2 tablespoons olive oil
400 g diced pork
1 tablespoon Middle Eastern
  spice booster (see page 123)
1 large red onion, chopped
600 g sweet potato, chopped
3 cups (750 ml) salt-reduced
  chicken stock
8 large kale leaves, white stalks
  removed, leaves torn
400 g tin chickpeas, drained
  and rinsed
360 g (2 cups) cooked quinoa
  (see page 99)
1 cup coriander sprigs (optional)

Heat the oil in a large, deep non-stick frying pan over medium heat. Add the pork, spice booster and onion and cook, stirring occasionally, for 5 minutes. Add the sweet potato and stock, then simmer, stirring occasionally, for 10 minutes.

Stir in the kale and chickpeas and simmer, stirring occasionally, for 5 minutes or until cooked through and the sauce has reduced by half. Season with freshly ground black pepper.

Divide the quinoa among serving bowls and spoon the stew over the top. Serve sprinkled with coriander, if desired.

UNITS PER SERVE • MEAT & ALT 1.5 • GRAIN 2 • VEGETABLES 3 • OIL 2

INDIAN SPICE
BOOSTER

ITALIAN SPICE
BOOSTER

MEXICAN SPICE
BOOSTER

ALL-PURPOSE
SPICE BOOSTER

ASIAN SPICE
BOOSTER

SPICES NOT ONLY
ADD FLAVOUR WITHOUT
THE NEED FOR SALT, BUT
THEY ALSO PROVIDE
AN IMPRESSIVE ARRAY
OF VITAMINS, MINERALS
AND PHYTONUTRIENTS.

Spice boosters

A spice booster can be used as a flavour base, dry rub or seasoning when you're cooking or making dressings, marinades, dips, salsas or sauces. Or sprinkle over your meal as a flavour enhancer just before serving. Mixing these yourself works out to be more economical and avoids the inclusion of extra salt.

Indian spice booster

Spices are the foundation of all Indian cooking and this combination will make your curries sing. Made with families in mind, we've omitted the chilli, but you can add it to your recipes to taste.

MAKES ABOUT ½ CUP
PREPARATION 5 MINUTES

3 tablespoons garam masala
1 tablespoon ground coriander
1 tablespoon ground cumin
2 teaspoons ground ginger
2 teaspoons ground turmeric

Place all the ingredients in a screw-top jar, seal and then shake until well combined. Store in a cool, dark place for up to 2 months.

Italian spice booster

This is the go-to seasoning blend for pasta sauces, but you can also sprinkle it on vegetables or potatoes for extra flavour, or mix it into salad dressings.

MAKES ABOUT ⅔ CUP
PREPARATION 5 MINUTES

2 tablespoons dried basil
2 tablespoons dried oregano
2 tablespoons dried marjoram
1 tablespoon dried thyme
1 tablespoon dried rosemary

Place all the ingredients in a screw-top jar, seal and then shake until well combined. Store in a cool, dark place for up to 2 months.

Mexican spice booster

If you don't like a lot of heat you can leave out the chilli powder. For those feeding young children, a good option is to make the spice blend without it, then add dried chilli to taste for those who want it in their meal.

MAKES ABOUT ⅔ CUP
PREPARATION 5 MINUTES

2 tablespoons sweet paprika
2 tablespoons smoked paprika
2 tablespoons ground cumin
2 tablespoons ground coriander
1–2 teaspoons chilli powder (optional)

Place all the ingredients in a screw-top jar, seal and then shake until well combined. Store in a cool, dark place for up to 2 months.

All-purpose spice booster

This flavour-enhancing mix will become your secret ingredient. It can be rubbed onto chicken or pork prior to pan-frying for a basic 'meat and 3 veg' meal or added to soups and casseroles, mashed potato and rice or any other side dish that needs a pop of flavour.

MAKES ABOUT ⅔ CUP
PREPARATION 5 MINUTES

3 tablespoons sweet paprika
2 tablespoons garlic powder
2 tablespoons onion powder
1 tablespoon dried parsley

Place all the ingredients in a screw-top jar, seal and then shake until well combined. Store in a cool, dark place for up to 2 months.

Asian spice booster

There are various lemon pepper blends available – be sure to select one that is made with plenty of dried mixed herbs and flavours such as capsicum, parsley, onion and garlic, and has minimal salt added.

MAKES ABOUT ½ CUP
PREPARATION 5 MINUTES

1 tablespoon onion powder
1 tablespoon garlic powder
2 tablespoons ground coriander
2 tablespoons ground cumin
2 teaspoons salt-reduced lemon pepper (see intro)

Place all the ingredients in a screw-top jar, seal and then shake until well combined. Store in a cool, dark place for up to 2 months.

Middle Eastern spice booster

This spice booster is also known as dukkah and can make a simple dish shine. You can sprinkle it over salad greens, soup or roasted vegetables, use it as a coating for fish, chicken or pork, serve on top of avocado toast or enjoy it simply with pita or crusty bread and a good-quality olive oil. If you don't have pistachios, feel free to replace them with hazelnuts or simply use more almonds.

MAKES ABOUT 1 CUP
PREPARATION 5 MINUTES

½ cup (80 g) almonds
⅓ cup (45 g) unsalted shelled pistachios
3 tablespoons sesame seeds
2 tablespoons cumin seeds
2 tablespoons coriander seeds
1 teaspoon fennel seeds (optional)

Preheat the oven to 180°C (160°C fan-forced).

Spread out the nuts and seeds on a baking tray and toast in the oven for about 5 minutes or dry pan-fry for 3–5 minutes. Stir frequently to prevent burning.

Cool, then blitz the nuts and seeds into crumbs in a food processor. Alternatively, grind with a mortar and pestle. Store in a cool, dark place for up to 2 months.

MIDDLE EASTERN SPICE BOOSTER

Simple spice-booster bowls

QUICK CHICKPEA
CURRY

MEXI-BOWL

PASTA TOSS

SALMON AND MASH

TOFU STIR-FRY

Simple spice-booster bowls

These main meals incorporate spice boosters for those times when you need a tasty dinner on the table quickly. First, get the grain or potatoes cooking. Then, simply heat the oil in a large, deep non-stick frying pan over medium–high heat. Add the spice booster and meat/alt and cook, tossing, for 2 minutes. Add the vegetables and cook, tossing occasionally, for 8–10 minutes or until cooked and golden. Spoon the grain or potatoes into serving dishes, top with the protein mixture and add the 'serve with' ingredients, if you're using them. And, of course, you can modify the ingredients to avoid wasting fresh produce or meat you already have.

EACH MEAL SERVES 4

Mexi-bowl

640 g (4 cups) cooked brown rice (page 99)
1 tablespoon olive oil
1 tablespoon Mexican spice booster (page 122)
600 g beef stir-fry strips
2 green capsicums and 1 red capsicum, seeded and sliced
3 zucchini, sliced
1 red onion, sliced
80 g sliced avocado

Serve with
lime wedges
coriander leaves

Quick chickpea curry

4 x 80 g wholemeal pita breads, split
1 tablespoon sunflower oil
1 tablespoon Indian spice booster (page 121)
3 x 400 g tins chickpeas, drained and rinsed
400 g baby green beans, trimmed
1 red onion, chopped
600 g peeled finely diced pumpkin
3 large tomatoes, chopped
2 tablespoons toasted slivered almonds, chopped

Serve with
coriander and mint leaves
lemon wedges

Pasta toss

640 g (4 cups) cooked wholegrain penne
2 tablespoons extra virgin olive oil
1 tablespoon Italian spice booster (page 121)
600 g diced chicken breast
600 g baby medley tomatoes, halved (or 5 vine-ripened tomatoes, chopped)
1 yellow capsicum, seeded and diced
150 g snow peas, sliced, or 160 g (1 cup) peas

Serve with
lemon wedges
basil leaves

UNITS PER SERVE · MEAT & ALT 1.5 · GRAIN 2 · VEGETABLES 3 · OIL 2

Tofu stir-fry

640 g (4 cups) soaked brown rice
    vermicelli noodles
2 tablespoons sunflower oil
1 tablespoon Asian spice booster
    (page 122)
1 kg firm tofu, cut into 2 cm pieces
500 g sugar snap peas, trimmed
4 spring onions, sliced
1 yellow capsicum, seeded
    and sliced

Serve with
1 bunch Chinese broccoli,
    trimmed, steamed
Thai basil leaves
lime wedges

Salmon and mash

1 tablespoon olive oil
1 tablespoon All-purpose spice
    booster (page 122)
600 g skinless, boneless salmon
    portions, cut into 2 cm pieces
1 red onion, cut into wedges
2 zucchini, sliced
2 sticks celery, sliced
1.2 kg boiled potatoes, mashed

Serve with
3 cups mixed salad leaves
80 g sliced avocado
flat-leaf parsley leaves
lemon wedges

TIP

Use the ideas on
page 83 to tailor recipes
to timid or adventurous
taste buds.

Lamb and eggplant rice

WEEKDAY DINNER

SERVES **4**
PREPARATION **25 MINUTES**
COOKING **15 MINUTES**

Beef strips can be used in place of lamb in this recipe and if you don't have (or don't like) eggplant, replace it with zucchini, squash or even asparagus, when they're in season. To make sure the meat is tender, let it come to room temperature first, ensure the pan is hot enough to seal the outside, and avoid overcooking.

2 large eggplants, cut into
   2 cm pieces
600 g lamb strips
1 tablespoon smoked paprika
olive oil cooking spray
4 roma tomatoes, cut into
   eighths lengthways
2 cups rocket leaves
80 g avocado, sliced
1 x quantity Mustard and lemon
   3-in-1 (see page 139)
640 g (4 cups) cooked brown
   basmati rice (see page 99)

Heat a large, deep non-stick frying pan over medium–high heat.

Combine the eggplant, lamb and paprika in a bowl and season with freshly ground black pepper. Toss well to combine, then spray lightly with oil.

Working in three batches, cook the lamb mixture for 4–5 minutes each or until just cooked and golden. Transfer to a large bowl.

Add all the remaining ingredients to the bowl and gently toss to combine. Season with freshly ground black pepper and serve.

UNITS PER SERVE • MEAT & ALT 1.5 • GRAIN 2 • VEGETABLES 3 • OIL 2

Beef and kidney bean fajitas

SERVES **4**
PREPARATION **25 MINUTES**
COOKING **10 MINUTES**

The fajitas can be topped with coriander leaves, a squeeze of lime juice, fresh or dried red chilli and a drizzle of natural yoghurt. The beef mixture is also delicious spooned over baked jacket potatoes or inside a toasted sandwich. In fact, it's so versatile you may want to double the quantities for an easy meal to be enjoyed later in the week.

1 tablespoon olive oil

400 g beef stir-fry strips or lean beef mince

400 g tin red kidney beans, drained and rinsed

3 capsicums (green, red and yellow, if possible), seeded and sliced

2 red onions, sliced

1 tablespoon Mexican spice booster (see page 122)

8 x 40 g multigrain soft wraps, warmed

240 g (4 cups) shredded iceberg lettuce

80 g mashed avocado

lime halves and coriander leaves, to serve

Heat the oil in a large, deep non-stick frying pan over high heat. Add the beef, beans, capsicum, onion and spice booster and cook, tossing, for 6–8 minutes or until the meat is tender and the vegetables are golden crisp.

Divide the wraps among serving plates. Top with the beef mixture, lettuce and avocado, then roll or fold up and serve with lime halves and coriander leaves.

UNITS PER SERVE • MEAT & ALT 1.5 • GRAIN 2 • VEGETABLES 3 • OIL 2

Spice-crusted pork fillet with roast apple salad

SERVES **4**
PREPARATION **20 MINUTES**
COOKING **30 MINUTES**

Chicken fillets can be used in place of pork, but may need to be cooked for a little longer so be careful not to burn the crust. Baby beetroot can be found with the other tinned vegetables or look for it vacuum-packed in the fresh vegetable section of most supermarkets.

600 g potatoes, cut into
   2 cm wedges
2 granny smith apples, cored
   and sliced into wedges
1 tablespoon honey
olive oil cooking spray
600 g pork fillet
½ x quantity Middle Eastern
   spice booster (see page 123)
2 x 400 g tins baby beetroot,
   drained and quartered
4 cups rocket leaves
1 tablespoon balsamic vinegar
lemon wedges, to serve

Preheat the oven to 200°C (180°C fan-forced). Line a baking tray with baking paper.

Place the potato and apple wedges on the prepared tray. Drizzle with honey and spray lightly with oil, then season to taste with freshly ground black pepper. Roast for 30 minutes or until the apple and potato are tender with a caramelised finish.

Meanwhile, spray the pork with oil and roll in the Middle Eastern spice booster until thickly covered. Spray a deep non-stick frying pan with oil and heat the pan over medium heat. Cook for 6 minutes on one side, then turn and cook for a further 3 minutes on the other side. Leave to rest for 5 minutes.

Slice the pork fillets into 1 cm thick slices and serve next to the baby beetroot and the potato and apple mix. Top with the rocket and balsamic vinegar, season with freshly ground black pepper and serve with lemon wedges.

UNITS PER SERVE • MEAT & ALT 1.5 • GRAIN 2
• VEGETABLES 3 • OIL 2 • FRUIT 0.5

Pepper steak with vegetable macaroni

SERVES **4**
PREPARATION **25 MINUTES**
COOKING **20 MINUTES**

Artichoke hearts can be found in jars in most supermarkets but if you don't have them in your pantry just add more of the other vegetables. Ever tried kohlrabi? It's a cross between broccoli and cabbage and would make an interesting addition to this dish. Just wash and dice one into small pieces and add it to the tomato mixture with the zucchini and capsicum.

1 ½ tablespoons extra virgin olive oil
400 g tin crushed tomatoes
½ x quantity Italian balsamic 3-in-1 (see page 138)
1 large red capsicum, seeded and sliced
2 zucchini, sliced
90 g (1 cup) drained artichoke hearts in brine
4 x 150 g beef steaks, generously seasoned with freshly ground black pepper
2 red onions, sliced into rings
640 g (4 cups) cooked macaroni
1 cup small flat-leaf parsley leaves

Place the oil and tomatoes in a saucepan over medium heat and cook, stirring occasionally, for 5 minutes or until thickened. Add the 3-in-1, capsicum, zucchini and artichokes. Reduce the heat to low and cook gently, stirring occasionally, for 10 minutes.

Meanwhile, heat a large chargrill pan over high heat.

Chargrill the beef and onion rings for 5 minutes for medium, turning only once, or cook to your liking. Divide among serving plates, then cover loosely and allow to rest.

Add the pasta and parsley to the tomato mixture and cook, stirring, for 2 minutes or until heated through and well combined. Serve alongside the steak and onion rings.

UNITS PER SERVE • MEAT & ALT 1.5 • GRAIN 2 • VEGETABLES 3 • OIL 2

Hoisin beef stir-fry

SERVES **4**
PREPARATION **20 MINUTES**
COOKING **10 MINUTES**

If you're under time pressure and don't have any precooked rice, use fresh noodles instead. Add extra vegetables for those with bigger appetites – capsicum (all colours), snow peas, mushrooms and green beans will work well in this stir-fry.

---

1 tablespoon sunflower oil
600 g beef stir-fry strips
1 tablespoon Asian spice booster
   (see page 122)
2 tablespoons hoisin sauce
2 spring onions, cut into
   3 cm lengths
2 bunches broccolini, cut into
   3 cm lengths
2 large sticks celery, sliced on
   an angle
1 bunch bok choy, sliced
640 g (4 cups) cooked brown rice
   (see page 99)

Combine the oil, beef, spice booster and hoisin in a bowl.

Heat a large wok over high heat. Stir-fry the beef mixture in three batches for 2 minutes each. Transfer to a bowl.

Add all the remaining ingredients to the wok, along with 3 tablespoons water. Stir-fry for 2 minutes or until the vegetables are almost tender and the rice is light golden and starting to crisp. Return the beef mixture to the wok, toss well and serve.

UNITS PER SERVE • **MEAT & ALT** 1.5 • **GRAIN** 2 • **VEGETABLES** 3 • **OIL** 2

3-in-1s

ITALIAN BALSAMIC

GARLIC CITRUS YOGHURT

SOY, SESAME AND GINGER

MUSTARD AND LEMON

TAHINI AND LIME

3-in-1s

Keep these go-to pantry and fridge staples on hand to use as marinades, dressings or sauces in your meals. A great tip is to have your chosen options made up on a Sunday night to give your midweek meals maximum flavour without you having to spend much time in the kitchen. Double the quantities for larger crowds.

Italian balsamic

SERVES **4**
PREPARATION **5 MINUTES**

1 tablespoon extra virgin olive oil
2 teaspoons Italian spice booster (see page 121)
½ cup (125 ml) balsamic vinegar
2 teaspoons brown sugar

Place all the ingredients in a screw-top jar, seal and then shake until well combined. Store in a cool, dark place for up to 5 days. Before using, shake well and season with freshly ground black pepper.

Garlic citrus yoghurt

SERVES **4**
PREPARATION **10 MINUTES**

200 g natural Greek-style yoghurt
2 teaspoons extra virgin olive oil
finely grated zest and juice of 2 medium oranges
1 clove garlic, crushed
2 tablespoons finely chopped chives

Place all the ingredients in a screw-top jar, seal and then shake until well combined. Store in the fridge for up to 5 days. Before using, shake well and season with freshly ground black pepper.

Soy, sesame and ginger

SERVES **4**
PREPARATION **10 MINUTES**

½ cup (125 ml) salt-reduced soy sauce
8 drops sesame oil
1 teaspoon Asian spice booster (see page 122)
2 cm piece ginger, finely grated

Place all the ingredients in a screw-top jar, seal and then shake until well combined. Store in the fridge for up to 5 days. Before using, shake well and season with freshly ground black pepper.

TAHINI IS A THICK PASTE MADE FROM SESAME SEEDS. IT'S USUALLY FOUND NEAR OTHER NUT BUTTERS IN THE SUPERMARKET.

↓

Tahini and lime

SERVES **4**
PREPARATION **10 MINUTES**

1 tablespoon tahini
finely grated zest and juice
    of 4 large limes
1 teaspoon Mexican spice
    booster (see page 122)
1 tablespoon finely
    chopped coriander

Using a fork, whisk the tahini, lime zest and juice, and spice booster in a screw-top jar until smooth and well combined. Seal and store in the fridge for up to 5 days.

Just before using, add the coriander and enough warm water (1–2 tablespoons) to loosen the mixture to a thick drizzle consistency. Season with freshly ground black pepper.

Mustard and lemon

SERVES **4**
PREPARATION **5 MINUTES**

1 tablespoon extra virgin
    olive oil
1 tablespoon wholegrain
    mustard
finely grated zest and juice
    of 2 lemons
2 teaspoons pure maple syrup

Place all the ingredients in a screw-top jar, seal and then shake until well combined. Store in the fridge for up to 5 days. Before using, shake well and season with freshly ground black pepper.

Meat-less lovers' pizza

WEEKDAY
DINNER

SERVES **4**
PREPARATION **25 MINUTES**
COOKING **25 MINUTES**

Quorn™ and other plant-based mince products can be found in the freezer section of the supermarket. If you want to include a final flourish of dairy, sprinkle feta over the cooked pizzas just before serving.

1 ½ tablespoons olive oil

600 g Quorn™ 'mince'
  or other plant-based mince

300 g mushrooms, sliced

2 x 80 g large wholemeal pita
  breads

3 tablespoons salt-reduced
  tomato paste

1 onion, very thinly sliced
  into rings

1 green capsicum, seeded
  and thinly sliced

4 cups mixed salad leaves

½ x quantity Italian balsamic
  3-in-1 (see page 138)

160 g feta (optional)

Preheat the oven to 200°C (180°C fan-forced). Line 2 large baking trays with baking paper.

Heat the oil in a large, deep non-stick frying pan over medium–high heat. Add the Quorn and cook, stirring and breaking up any large pieces with a spoon, for 3 minutes. Add the mushroom and cook, stirring occasionally, for 3 minutes or until softened and golden and the mixture in the pan is dry.

Spread one side of each pita bread with tomato paste and transfer to the prepared trays. Top evenly with the Quorn mixture, then the onion and capsicum. Place both trays in the oven and bake for 15–18 minutes, swapping the trays around halfway through, until the bases are crisp and the tops are golden.

Toss the leaves with the 3-in-1 dressing in a bowl, then arrange on the pizzas. Sprinkle with crumbled feta (if using) and serve hot.

UNITS PER SERVE • MEAT & ALT 1.5 • GRAIN 2 • VEGETABLES 3 • OIL 2

Vietnamese fried rice with egg

WEEKDAY
DINNER

SERVES **4**
PREPARATION **15 MINUTES**
COOKING **10 MINUTES**

Bean sprouts don't stay fresh for long. When planning your meals for the week ahead, schedule this one for soon after shopping day. Frozen vegetables are a cost-effective and handy alternative to fresh. Having packets of peas, corn, beans, spinach and broad beans in the freezer will ensure you always have options available. Another bonus: they shave a bit of time off your meal prep.

---

1 tablespoon sunflower oil

4 eggs, whisked

650 g firm tofu, finely diced

300 g green beans, trimmed
    and halved

640 g (4 cups) cooked brown rice
    (see page 99)

120 g (1 cup) frozen baby peas

1 x quantity Soy, sesame and
    ginger 3-in-1 (see page 138)

4 spring onions, sliced

160 g (2 cups) bean sprouts

Heat half the oil in a large non-stick wok over high heat. Add the egg and scramble constantly for 1–2 minutes or until cooked. Transfer to a plate.

Heat the remaining oil in the wok over high heat. Add the tofu and beans and stir-fry for 2 minutes. Toss in the rice and stir-fry for 2 minutes or until dry and starting to crisp. Add the peas and cook for 2 minutes or until heated through. Pour in the 3-in-1 and toss until well combined. Remove the wok from the heat.

Return the egg to the wok, along with the spring onion and bean sprouts. Season with freshly ground black pepper, then give everything a final toss to combine before serving.

UNITS PER SERVE • **MEAT & ALT** 1.5 • **GRAIN** 2 • **VEGETABLES** 3 • **OIL** 2

Roast vegetables with bean salsa

SERVES **4**
PREPARATION **25 MINUTES**
COOKING **25 MINUTES**

Almost any vegetable is delicious roasted. Do you have a head of broccoli that is looking a little unloved, or a bag of carrots that didn't quite make it into the weekly meal rotation? Chop up, toss in a drizzle of oil and your favourite spice booster (see page 121) and roast using the method below. These are perfect for snacks, as a side dish, mixed into salads or added to a breakfast hash.

800 g peeled pumpkin, cut into small wedges
1 small head cauliflower, florets separated, stems roughly chopped
olive oil cooking spray
1 x quantity Tahini and lime 3-in-1 (see page 139)
2 x 400 g tins black beans, drained and rinsed
2 x 400 g tins red kidney beans, drained and rinsed
2 large tomatoes, finely diced
2 Lebanese cucumbers, finely diced
1 red onion, finely chopped
1 cup flat-leaf parsley leaves
4 x 80 g wholemeal pita breads, torn

Preheat the oven to 220°C (200°C fan-forced). Line a large baking tray with baking paper.

Place the pumpkin and cauliflower on the prepared tray and spread out in a single layer. Spray lightly with oil and season with freshly ground black pepper. Roast for 20–25 minutes or until cooked and golden.

Meanwhile, combine all the remaining ingredients (except the pita bread) in a large bowl. Season with freshly ground black pepper.

Add the hot roasted vegetables to the bean mixture and toss to combine. Serve warm with the pita bread alongside.

UNITS PER SERVE • MEAT & ALT 1.5 • GRAIN 2 • VEGETABLES 3+ • OIL 1

Quorn™ and mushroom bolognese

SERVES **4**
PREPARATION **25 MINUTES**
COOKING **20 MINUTES**

For a non-vegetarian meal, use beef mince or try half beef and half plant-based mince. As an alternative to the baby spinach, try adding a large bunch of chopped flat-leaf parsley at the end of cooking.

2 tablespoons olive oil
600 g Quorn™ 'mince'
   or other plant-based mince
1 large onion, finely diced
2 large carrots, finely diced
2 sticks celery, finely diced
300 g cup mushrooms, sliced
3 teaspoons Italian spice booster
   (see page 121)
2 x 400 g tins crushed tomatoes
2 cups baby spinach leaves
640 g (4 cups) cooked
   wholegrain spaghetti

Heat the oil in a large, deep non-stick frying pan over medium–high heat. Add the Quorn and cook, stirring and breaking up any large pieces with a spoon, for 3 minutes. Add the onion, carrot, celery and mushroom and cook, stirring occasionally, for 2 minutes or until light golden and starting to soften.

Reduce the heat to medium–low. Add the spice booster and tomatoes and cook, stirring occasionally, for 15 minutes or until the vegetables are tender and the sauce has reduced by three-quarters. Remove the pan from the heat, stir in the spinach and let it wilt.

Divide the spaghetti among serving plates, spoon over the bolognese and serve.

UNITS PER SERVE • MEAT & ALT 1.5 • GRAIN 2 • VEGETABLES 3 • OIL 2

Herbed greens and lentil penne

SERVES **4**
PREPARATION **25 MINUTES**
COOKING **20 MINUTES**

You don't have to be vegetarian to include regular meat-free meals in your repertoire – this is known as a 'flexitarian' way of eating. Try this recipe on a 'Meat-free Monday'!

2 tablespoons olive oil

finely grated zest and juice of
   2 lemons

1 bunch basil, leaves picked

1 cup baby rocket leaves

2 spring onions, sliced

1 clove garlic, crushed

1 teaspoon Italian spice booster
   (see page 121)

3 x 400 g tins lentils, drained
   and rinsed

4 cups baby spinach leaves

640 g (4 cups) cooked
   wholegrain penne

Place the oil, lemon zest and juice, basil, rocket, spring onion, garlic and spice booster in a food processor and blend until smooth, adding a little water, if needed, to loosen. Season with freshly ground black pepper.

Transfer the pesto to a large bowl. Add the lentils, baby spinach and penne, season with freshly ground black pepper and toss to combine. Serve.

UNITS PER SERVE • MEAT & ALT 1.5 • GRAIN 2 • VEGETABLES 2+ • OIL 2

RAW AND ROASTED

COLOUR AND CRUNCH

Easy salads

It's easy to toss together a salad using a base of fresh and/or cooked vegetables, then dress it up with a 3-in-1 dressing (see page 138) and a few toppings. Serve it with protein such as fish, chicken or beef and a side of either rice, pasta or potato and you have an almost instant meal – possibly faster than a takeaway!

Raw and roasted

Base

Any combination of fresh salad greens and mixed roasted vegetables (see page 144)

3-in-1 dressing

Mustard and lemon (see page 139)

Optional toppings

Toasted seeds

Serve with ...

Grilled haloumi and basil

Colour and crunch

Base
Any combination of shredded
    carrot, white cabbage, red
    cabbage and snow peas

3-in-1 dressing
Soy, sesame and ginger
    (see page 138)

Optional toppings
Crushed unsalted peanuts, mint
    and/or coriander

Serve with ...
Stir-fried beef strips and
    steamed rice

Bitter sweet

Base
Shaved fennel, thinly sliced pear
    and radicchio

3-in-1 dressing
Garlic citrus yoghurt
    (see page 138)

Optional toppings
Shaved parmesan

Serve with ...
Pan-seared salmon

Greek goddess

Base
Mixed salad greens, sliced
    tomato, cucumber and
    red capsicum

3-in-1 dressing
Italian balsamic (see page 138)

Optional toppings
Feta and olives

Serve with ...
BBQ chicken

BITTER SWEET

GREEK GODDESS

Roast broccoli, chickpea and quinoa salad

SERVES **4**
PREPARATION **20 MINUTES**
COOKING **25 MINUTES**

Tempeh is similar to tofu in that they are both made from soy beans. However, tempeh has a heartier flavour and firmer texture, making it a particularly good alternative to meat.

---

2 heads broccoli, florets
    separated, stems chopped
2 x 400 g tins chickpeas, drained,
    rinsed and patted dry
340 g tempeh, cut into
    2 cm cubes
1 tablespoon Indian spice
    booster (see page 121)
olive oil cooking spray
80 g avocado, chopped
1 x quantity Mustard and lemon
    3-in-1 (see page 139)
720 g (4 cups) cooked quinoa
    (see page 99)

Preheat the oven to 220°C (200°C fan-forced). Line a large baking tray with baking paper.

Place the broccoli, chickpeas, tempeh and spice booster on the prepared tray. Toss to combine and coat well, then spread out in a single layer. Spray lightly with oil and season with freshly ground black pepper.

Roast for 20–25 minutes or until cooked and golden crisp.

Transfer the roast vegetable mixture to a large bowl, add the avocado, 3-in-1 and quinoa and toss to combine. Serve warm.

UNITS PER SERVE • MEAT & ALT 1.5 • GRAIN 2 • VEGETABLES 3 • OIL 2

Tofu steaks with cabbage and pea slaw

SERVES **4**
PREPARATION **25 MINUTES**
COOKING **20 MINUTES**

A great option for an easy meat-free weeknight dinner. You might want to use a little less tofu, depending on your appetite. If you don't use a whole packet, leftover tofu can be safely stored in a container with fresh water in the fridge for up to 3 days.

olive oil cooking spray
4 zucchini, sliced lengthways
2 tablespoons All-purpose spice booster (see page 122)
1 kg firm tofu, cut into 16 slices

Cabbage and pea slaw
1 tablespoon extra virgin olive oil
2 tablespoons red wine vinegar
1 teaspoon brown sugar
600 g red cabbage, shredded
2 spring onions, thinly sliced
240 g (2 cups) frozen baby peas, thawed
2 tablespoons toasted flaked almonds

To make the cabbage and pea slaw, whisk together the oil, vinegar and sugar in a large bowl until the sugar has dissolved. Add the remaining ingredients, season with freshly ground black pepper and toss to combine and coat in the dressing. Set aside.

Lightly spray a large non-stick frying pan with oil and heat over medium heat. Add the zucchini in three batches and cook for 5 minutes each or until tender and golden. Transfer to plates.

Reheat the pan over medium heat. Sprinkle the spice booster over both sides of the tofu and spray with oil. Place in the pan and cook, turning occasionally, for 5 minutes or until heated through and golden crisp.

Add the tofu to the plates and serve with the cabbage and pea slaw alongside.

UNITS PER SERVE • **MEAT & ALT** 1.5 • **VEGETABLES** 3+ • **OIL** 2

weekday sweet

Vanilla-stewed fruit
with yoghurt

SERVES **4**
PREPARATION **25 MINUTES,**
PLUS COOLING TIME
COOKING **15 MINUTES**

Poaching is a fantastic way to 'glam up' a healthy fruit dessert. You might also like to try rhubarb in this recipe, but keep in mind it will only need 5 minutes in the poaching liquid.

3 pink lady apples, cored
   and sliced or quartered
3 firm ripe pears, cored
   and sliced or quartered
30 g currants
1 teaspoon pure vanilla extract
800 g natural Greek-style
   yoghurt
2 tablespoons sunflower seeds
2 tablespoons toasted flaked
   almonds

Combine the apple, pear, currants, vanilla and 500 ml (2 cups) water in a saucepan over medium heat. Simmer, stirring occasionally, for 12–15 minutes or until the fruit is very soft and the liquid has reduced by three-quarters. Remove from the heat and either cool completely in the pan, or let it cool for 10 minutes if you want to serve it warm.

Spoon the yoghurt and stewed fruit into bowls or onto a serving platter. Sprinkle with sunflower seeds and almonds and serve.

UNITS PER SERVE • DAIRY 1 • FRUIT 1.5 • OIL 2

IN SUMMER, USE THIS METHOD FOR POACHING STONE FRUITS, SUCH AS NECTARINES AND PEACHES. KEEP IN THE FRIDGE AND SERVE CHILLED.

Passionfruit chia yoghurt 'jellies'

SERVES **4**
PREPARATION **15 MINUTES, PLUS
STANDING AND CHILLING TIME**

If passionfruit is not in season you can replace it with other fruit, such as ¾ cup frozen mango or mixed berries – keep in mind that extra juice from the fruit might be needed for the chia to absorb. You can easily make a double or even triple batch of these jellies. Store them in an airtight container in the fridge for up to 4 days.

2 tablespoons chia seeds
pulp of 8 passionfruit
800 g natural Greek-style
  yoghurt
1 teaspoon pure vanilla extract
2 tablespoon mixed seeds
  (pumpkin seeds/pepitas,
  sunflower seeds)
2 teaspoons mint leaves

In a bowl, combine the chia seeds and most of the passionfruit pulp, reserving a little passionfruit to serve. Leave for about 10 minutes, stirring occasionally, until the chia plumps up. Stir in the yoghurt and vanilla, then divide the mixture evenly among serving glasses.

Chill for at least 4 hours, or overnight if time permits, until set to a jelly. Sprinkle with seeds and mint and serve with the reserved passionfruit.

UNITS PER SERVE • DAIRY 1 • FRUIT 1 • OIL 2

Baked berry custard

WEEKDAY
SWEET

SERVES **4**
PREPARATION **20 MINUTES**
COOKING **15 MINUTES**

We've used strawberries and raspberries here but you could just as easily make this with other varieties – try blackberries, blueberries or mixed berries (fresh or frozen).

500 g strawberries, hulled
and halved
300 g raspberries
300 g fresh ricotta
200 ml custard
½ teaspoon ground nutmeg
1 teaspoon icing sugar
2 tablespoons toasted pumpkin
seeds (pepitas)

Preheat the oven to 210°C (190°C fan-forced).

Combine the strawberries and raspberries in a 20 cm round pie plate, covering the base evenly.

Using a fork, whisk together the ricotta, custard and nutmeg until smooth. Dollop over the berries and bake for 12–15 minutes or until golden and the berries start to release their juices.

Serve warm, dusted with icing sugar and sprinkled with pumpkin seeds.

UNITS PER SERVE • DAIRY 1 • FRUIT 1 • OIL 1

Saffron oranges and prunes with yoghurt

SERVES **4**
PREPARATION **20 MINUTES,
PLUS STANDING TIME**

This is a creative way to serve fruit for dessert in winter. If you don't have saffron, no problem – use ¼ teaspoon ground turmeric instead. And, by the way, 'macerate' is just a fancy word for 'soften by soaking in a liquid'!

---

800 g natural Greek-style
   yoghurt
6 oranges, zest finely grated,
   oranges peeled and sliced
   into ½ cm-thick rounds
1 teaspoon pure vanilla extract
60 g pitted soft prunes,
   finely chopped
pinch saffron threads
2 tablespoons toasted
   slivered almonds

Place the yoghurt in a bowl and stir through the orange zest. Cover and chill while you prepare the fruit.

Combine the orange slices, vanilla, prunes and saffron in a bowl. Set aside to macerate at room temperature for 20 minutes.

Divide the orange yoghurt among serving bowls and top with the orange and prune mixture. Sprinkle with the almonds and serve.

UNITS PER SERVE • DAIRY 1 • FRUIT 1 • OIL 1

Tropical salsa with ginger ricotta cream

WEEKDAY SWEET

SERVES 4
PREPARATION 30 MINUTES

Transport yourself to a tropical location with this sweet and refreshing dessert. You could add some toasted flaked coconut on top for an even more intense tropical experience, either in place of or together with the nuts.

4 small kiwifruit, finely chopped

320 g (2 cups) finely chopped pineapple

320 g (2 cups) finely chopped seedless watermelon

2 tablespoons mint leaves

240 g fresh ricotta

400 g natural Greek-style yoghurt

1 cm piece ginger, finely chopped

1 teaspoon pure vanilla extract

2 tablespoons finely chopped roasted, unsalted mixed nuts (walnuts, almonds, Brazil nuts)

Combine the fruit and mint in a bowl. Set aside while you prepare the ricotta cream.

Using an electric hand-held mixer, beat together the ricotta, yoghurt, ginger and vanilla until smooth.

Divide the ricotta cream among serving bowls and spoon over the fruit mixture. Sprinkle with nuts and serve.

UNITS PER SERVE • DAIRY 1 • FRUIT 1 • OIL 1

Banana blueberry nice-cream bites

SERVES **4 (MAKES 16)**
PREPARATION **25 MINUTES,**
PLUS FREEZING TIME

This healthy alternative to regular ice-cream is the perfect snack on a warm summer's day. Keep some ripe bananas, peeled and sliced, in your freezer so you always have them ready for nice-cream. Slow the ripening of bananas by storing them away from other produce, especially avocados and pears.

4 medium bananas, sliced
  and frozen
800 g natural Greek-style
  yoghurt
2 teaspoons honey
2 teaspoons pure vanilla extract
600 g blueberries (fresh
  or frozen)
2 tablespoons finely chopped
  roasted, unsalted mixed nuts
  (walnuts, almonds, Brazil nuts)

Double-line a 20 cm x 18 cm x 5 cm deep slice tin with baking paper.

Using a stick blender or upright blender, blitz the banana, yoghurt, honey and vanilla until smooth. Spoon into the prepared tin and level the surface. Top with the blueberries, pressing them halfway down into the banana mixture, then sprinkle with the mixed nuts. Cover with plastic film and freeze for 4–6 hours or until set firm.

Remove the nice-cream from the freezer and leave for 5 minutes. Cut into 16 even 'bites' and serve immediately.

UNITS PER SERVE • DAIRY 1 • FRUIT 2 • OIL 1

week

ends

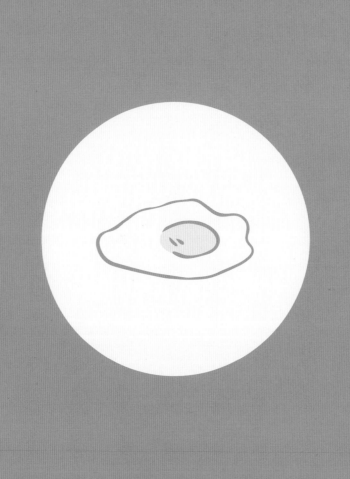

weekend brunch

Banana smoothie bowl

SERVES **4**
PREPARATION **15 MINUTES**

This is a nutritious way to use bananas that have been sitting in the fruit bowl a little too long. Save your over-ripe bananas by peeling, chopping and storing them in a ziplock bag or plastic container in the freezer until you are ready to use them.

8 medium over-ripe bananas, sliced, then frozen
800 g natural Greek-style yoghurt
1 tablespoon chia seeds
1 teaspoon mixed spice
1 ½ tablespoons pumpkin seeds (pepitas)
2 tablespoons toasted walnuts, chopped
½ cup mint leaves

Using an upright blender, blend the banana, yoghurt, chia and mixed spice until very smooth.

Divide the banana mixture among bowls and sprinkle with pumpkin seeds, walnuts and mint leaves. Serve immediately.

UNITS PER SERVE • DAIRY 1 • FRUIT 2 • OIL 2

Sardine bruschetta

SERVES 4
**PREPARATION 20 MINUTES,
PLUS STANDING TIME**

Did you know it's recommended that we consume two to three servings of fish per week? Oily fish, such as sardines and salmon, are particularly high in healthy omega-3 fats. This recipe makes a great lunch option, too.

---

4 large vine-ripened
    tomatoes, diced
½ quantity Italian balsamic 3-in-1
    (see page 138)
1 cup basil leaves, torn
4 x 40 g slices rye
    sourdough, toasted
1 clove garlic, halved
160 g grated mozzarella
1 ½ tablespoons extra virgin
    olive oil
400 g drained tinned sardines,
    lightly crushed

Combine the tomatoes, 3-in-1 and basil in a bowl and season with freshly ground black pepper. Set aside for 20 minutes to macerate, stirring occasionally.

Rub the warm toast with the cut sides of the garlic, then top with the mozzarella and let it melt a little. Arrange on serving plates and drizzle evenly with the oil. Top with the sardines and season with freshly ground black pepper, then spoon over the tomato mixture and serve.

UNITS PER SERVE • MEAT & ALT 1 • GRAIN 1 • VEG 1 • DAIRY 1 • OIL 2

Spinach and ricotta egg muffins

SERVES 4 (MAKES 8)
PREPARATION 25 MINUTES,
PLUS STANDING TIME
COOKING 25 MINUTES

The muffins will be quite puffy when they come out of the oven but will deflate slightly on cooling. This recipe doubles well and is freezer friendly too. Consider making a big batch so that you have a go-to breakfast for busy weekday mornings.

1 tablespoon olive oil
1 bunch silverbeet, white cores removed, leaves finely chopped
1 clove garlic, crushed
¼ teaspoon freshly grated nutmeg
8 large eggs, whisked
100 g natural Greek-style yoghurt
150 g fresh ricotta
4 x 40 g slices multigrain sourdough, toasted

Preheat the oven to 180°C (160°C fan-forced). Double line 8 holes of a 12-hole, ⅓ cup muffin tin with thick paper cases.

Heat the oil in a large, deep frying pan over high heat. Add the silverbeet and cook, tossing, for 2 minutes or until starting to wilt. Add the garlic and cook, stirring, for 1 minute or until the silverbeet has completely wilted and the mixture is dry. Transfer to a bowl, season with freshly ground black pepper and leave to cool for 5 minutes.

Add the nutmeg, egg, yoghurt and ricotta to the silverbeet mixture and stir until well combined.

Spoon the mixture evenly into the prepared muffin holes and bake for 18–20 minutes or until cooked and golden. Leave in the tin for 3 minutes, then remove and serve hot with toast.

UNITS PER SERVE • MEAT & ALT 1 • GRAIN 1 • VEG 0.5 • DAIRY 1 • OIL 1

Boiled egg and black bean bowls

SERVES **4**
PREPARATION **20 MINUTES**
COOKING **5 MINUTES**

Freekeh is wheat that has been harvested early, while the grains are still tender and green. It has long been popular in Middle Eastern cuisine and now Australians are embracing this nutritious grain. You can make a double batch of this recipe (without the eggs or avocado) and store it in an airtight container in the fridge for up to 3 days.

400 g tin black beans, drained
   and rinsed
1 bunch chives, finely chopped
1 green capsicum, seeded and
   finely chopped
4 cups baby spinach leaves
720 g (2 cups) cooked freekeh
   (see page 99)
80 g sliced avocado
1 cup flat-leaf parsley leaves
finely grated zest and juice of
   2 limes
4 large eggs
80 g sharp, mature cheddar,
   crumbled (optional)

Combine the black beans, chives, capsicum, baby spinach, freekeh, avocado, parsley, lime zest and juice in a bowl. Season with freshly ground black pepper and set aside.

Place the eggs in a saucepan of water and bring to the boil over high heat. Boil for 3–4 minutes for a soft centre or until cooked to your liking. Carefully remove, cool and peel the eggs, then cut them in half.

Divide the black bean mixture among bowls and top with the halved eggs. If using, sprinkle with the crumbled cheese and serve.

UNITS PER SERVE • MEAT & ALT 1 • GRAIN 1 • VEG 1 • DAIRY 1 • OIL 1

Breakfast tuna and haloumi toss

SERVES **4**
PREPARATION **15 MINUTES**
COOKING **5 MINUTES**

Haloumi has a high melting point, making it ideal for frying or grilling. It also has a higher salt content than other cheeses so enjoy it only occasionally. To reduce the salt content of the haloumi, place the slices in a bowl of water for 30 minutes, then drain and pat dry before use.

400 g drained tinned tuna
    chunks in springwater
1 x quantity Tahini and lime 3-in-1
    (see page 139)
1 tablespoon olive oil
1 teaspoon sweet paprika
400 g (2 cups) corn kernels
160 g haloumi, cut into
    1 cm cubes
6 large kale leaves, stalks
    removed, leaves torn

Combine the tuna and 3-in-1 in a large bowl. Season with freshly ground black pepper and set aside.

Heat the oil in a large, deep non-stick frying pan over high heat. Add the paprika, corn and haloumi and cook, tossing, for 2–3 minutes or until light golden. Add the kale and cook, tossing, for 1–2 minutes or until just starting to wilt.

Transfer the corn mixture to the bowl and toss with the tuna to combine. Serve warm.

UNITS PER SERVE • MEAT & ALT 1 • DAIRY 1 • VEGETABLES 1 • OIL 1

Mixed veggie hash with fried eggs

SERVES 4
PREPARATION 20 MINUTES
COOKING 15 MINUTES

This is a wonderful alternative to the traditional egg, bacon and potato hash breakfast. You may like to double the quantities and save some for later.

1 tablespoon olive oil

600 g potatoes, skins scrubbed, cut into small cubes (no larger than 1 cm)

2 onions, chopped

2 zucchini, chopped

200 g small button mushrooms, chopped

2 tablespoons thyme leaves

2 cups baby spinach leaves

olive oil cooking spray

8 large eggs

Heat the oil in a large, deep non-stick frying pan over medium heat. Add the potato, onion, zucchini and mushroom and cook, stirring occasionally, for 12–15 minutes or until the vegetables are cooked and golden crisp. Remove the pan from the heat. Add the thyme and spinach and season with freshly ground black pepper. Toss to combine well and set aside.

Meanwhile, lightly spray a separate large non-stick frying pan with oil and heat over medium–high heat. Working in two batches, crack in the eggs and cook for 3–4 minutes or until the whites have set firm, the edges are crispy and the yolks are still runny in the centre.

Divide the veggie hash among plates, top with the eggs and serve.

UNITS PER SERVE • MEAT & ALT 1 • GRAIN 1 • VEGETABLES 2 • OIL 1

Soft tofu shakshuka

SERVES **4**
PREPARATION **20 MINUTES**
COOKING **20 MINUTES**

Shakshuka is an easy breakfast (or brunch!) recipe eaten in Israel and other parts of the Middle East and North Africa. For a non-vegan option add 160 g crumbled Danish feta to the dish just before serving. You could also crack eggs into the pan instead of tofu.

---

2 x 400 g tins crushed tomatoes
2 teaspoons Italian spice booster (see page 121)
2 teaspoons smoked paprika
2 red capsicums, seeded and finely chopped
2 zucchini, finely chopped
680 g soft tofu, cut into 12 pieces
2 spring onions, thinly sliced
1 tablespoon toasted mixed seeds (sunflower seeds, linseeds, pumpkin seeds/pepitas)
4 x 40 g slices wholemeal bread, toasted
lemon wedges, to serve

Place the tomatoes, spice booster, paprika, capsicum, zucchini and 125 ml (½ cup) water in a large, deep non-stick frying pan over medium heat. Bring to a simmer and cook, stirring occasionally, for 10–12 minutes or until the vegetables are cooked and the liquid has reduced by one-third.

Gently press the tofu pieces halfway into the tomato mixture, then cover and cook for 5 minutes or until the tofu is heated through. Sprinkle with the spring onion and mixed seeds, then take the pan straight to the table and serve with toast alongside.

UNITS PER SERVE • MEAT & ALT 1 • GRAIN 1 • VEGETABLES 2 • OIL 1

weekend lunch

Smoked salmon and pea frittata with rocket and tomato salad

WEEKEND
LUNCH

SERVES **4**
PREPARATION **25 MINUTES,
PLUS RESTING TIME**
COOKING **25 MINUTES**

Tomatoes are best stored at room temperature, but away from sunlight. Pop them in the fruit bowl to let the sweet flavours develop for a few days before eating. Just remember they will ripen faster in the warmth of summer.

6 large eggs
400 g cottage cheese
2 tablespoons chopped dill
finely grated zest and juice of
   1 small lemon
100 g smoked salmon, chopped
240 g (2 cups) frozen baby
   peas, thawed
4 x 40 g slices wholegrain
   bread, toasted

Rocket and tomato salad
3 cups rocket leaves
2 sticks celery, thinly sliced,
   plus a few leaves
300 g baby medley tomatoes,
   halved or quartered
80 g sliced avocado
2 tablespoons toasted
   pecans, chopped
2 tablespoons white
   wine vinegar

Preheat the oven to 180°C (160°C fan-forced). Line a 20 cm square baking tin with baking paper.

In a large bowl, whisk together the eggs, cottage cheese, dill, lemon zest and juice until well combined. Stir in the smoked salmon and peas and season with freshly ground black pepper. Pour the mixture into the prepared tin and level the surface.

Bake for 20–25 minutes or until golden and set in the middle. Rest in the tin for 5 minutes before removing to slice.

Meanwhile, to make the rocket and tomato salad, combine all the ingredients in a bowl.

Cut the frittata into four pieces and divide among plates. Add the salad and serve warm with the toast alongside.

UNITS PER SERVE • **MEAT & ALT** 1 • **GRAIN** 1 • **VEG** 3 • **DAIRY** 1 • **OIL** 2

Hearty bean soup with roasted zucchini chips

SERVES **4**
PREPARATION **25 MINUTES**
COOKING **30 MINUTES**

Short on time? Just add the zucchini to the soup instead of baking it in the oven. This soup is great to have ready in the fridge for when hunger hits during the week.

4 zucchini, cut into
   1 cm-thick chips
1 tablespoon Italian spice
   booster (see page 121)
2 tablespoons olive oil
2 large onions, thinly sliced
2 sticks celery, chopped
2 carrots, chopped
2 x 400 g tins cannellini beans,
   drained and rinsed
2 cloves garlic, crushed
1.5 litres salt-reduced
   vegetable stock
1 bunch English spinach, leaves
   picked and chopped
4 x 40 g slices rye sourdough,
   toasted, cut into fingers

Preheat the oven to 220°C (200°C fan-forced). Line a large baking tray with baking paper.

Toss together the zucchini, spice booster and 1 tablespoon oil. Spread in a single layer on the tray and bake for 25–30 minutes or until cooked and golden.

Meanwhile, heat the remaining oil in a large saucepan over medium heat. Add the onion, celery and carrot and cook, stirring occasionally, for 15 minutes or until very tender and golden. Add the beans, garlic and stock and simmer, stirring occasionally, for 10 minutes or until the liquid has reduced slightly. Remove the pan from the heat, then stir in the spinach until it wilts. Season with freshly ground black pepper.

Ladle the soup into large bowls and serve with the zucchini chips and toast fingers.

UNITS PER SERVE • MEAT & ALT 1 • GRAIN 2 • VEGETABLES 3+ • OIL 2

Horseradish steak sandwiches with roast vegetables

SERVES **4**
PREPARATION **30 MINUTES**
COOKING **45 MINUTES**

Horseradish cream in a jar can be found in the condiments section of most supermarkets. Sizzle steaks are also known as minute steaks – they only take a minute to cook! Leftover roast beef would also work well in these sandwiches.

1 bunch beetroot
½ medium head cauliflower,
   florets separated,
   stem chopped
2 red onions, sliced into
   1 cm-thick rings
½ x quantity Italian balsamic
   3-in-1 (see page 138)
8 x 40 g slices rye sourdough
3 teaspoons horseradish cream
120 g mashed avocado
400 g beef sizzle steaks
2 vine-ripened tomatoes, sliced
1 baby cos lettuce,
   leaves separated

Preheat the oven to 210°C (190°C fan-forced). Line a large baking tray with baking paper.

Pick the leaves from the beetroot and give them a wash, then set aside for serving. Discard the stems and cut the beetroot bulbs in quarters.

Toss together the beetroot, cauliflower, onion and 3-in-1 in a bowl and season with freshly ground black pepper. Spread out evenly on the prepared tray and roast for 35–40 minutes, turning occasionally, until cooked and golden crisp. Remove from the oven and set aside.

Heat a large chargrill pan over high heat.

Chargrill the sourdough for 30–60 seconds or until lightly charred on both sides. Transfer to serving plates. Spread four pieces of toast with the horseradish and avocado. Season with freshly ground black pepper.

Chargrill the beef steaks for 30–60 seconds each side until cooked and lightly charred. Place on the toast and top with the tomato and cos leaves. Top with the remaining slices of toast, then cut in half crossways. Serve with the roast vegetables.

UNITS PER SERVE • MEAT & ALT 1.5 • GRAIN 2 • VEGETABLES 3+ • OIL 2

French toast with fresh tomato sauce

SERVES **4**
PREPARATION **15 MINUTES,
PLUS STANDING TIME**
COOKING **20 MINUTES**

French toast is a favourite weekend treat, but this version will also give you some serves of healthy grains and vegetables. The tomato sauce can be made in advance and stored in the fridge for up to 3 days.

8 large eggs
8 x 40 g slices multigrain bread
1 ½ tablespoons olive oil
1 bunch English spinach, leaves
    picked and torn

Fresh tomato sauce
6 roma tomatoes, finely chopped
2 teaspoons Italian spice booster
    (see page 121)
1 x quantity Mustard and lemon
    3-in-1 (see page 139)
1 cup flat-leaf parsley leaves

To make the fresh tomato sauce, combine all the ingredients in a bowl. Set aside for at least 30 minutes to macerate.

Whisk the eggs in a large flat dish and season with freshly ground black pepper. Add the bread slices, turning to coat well in the egg, then leave, turning occasionally, for 15 minutes or until all the egg has been absorbed.

Heat the oil in a large non-stick frying pan over medium heat. Working in batches, add the eggy bread and cook, turning once, for 8–10 minutes or until cooked and golden on both sides. Transfer to serving plates.

Reheat the pan over high heat. Add the spinach and cook, tossing, for 1–2 minutes or until starting to wilt. Spoon onto the French toast slices, and serve with the fresh tomato sauce alongside.

UNITS PER SERVE • MEAT & ALT 1 • GRAIN 2 • VEGETABLES 2+ • OIL 2

Roast chicken and pumpkin couscous salad

SERVES **4**
PREPARATION **30 MINUTES,
PLUS STANDING TIME**
COOKING **25 MINUTES**

If Brussels sprouts are not in season, use snow peas, blanched green beans or broad beans instead. Couscous is a staple of North African cooking and works well in this recipe, but if you don't have it on hand, brown rice or quinoa are delicious alternatives.

400 g chicken tenderloins

600 g peeled pumpkin, cut into 1 cm-thick slices

3 teaspoons All-purpose spice booster (see page 122)

olive oil cooking spray

200 g (1 cup) wholegrain couscous

375 ml (1 ½ cups) salt-reduced chicken stock, heated

1 bunch small radishes, thinly sliced into rounds

300 g Brussels sprouts, trimmed and shredded

200 g baby bocconcini, torn

2 tablespoons toasted Brazil nuts, chopped

1 x quantity Mustard and lemon 3-in-1 (see page 139)

Preheat the oven to 210°C (190°C fan-forced). Line a large baking tray with baking paper.

Toss together the chicken, pumpkin and spice booster in a bowl, then spread evenly over the prepared tray. Spray lightly with oil and roast for 20–25 minutes or until cooked and golden.

Meanwhile, place the couscous in a large bowl and pour over the hot stock. Cover and stand, untouched, for 10 minutes or until the couscous has absorbed the liquid and the grains are tender. Use a fork to fluff up the grains and season with freshly ground black pepper.

Add the roast chicken and pumpkin to the couscous and toss well to combine. Toss through the remaining ingredients and season with black pepper. Divide among bowls and serve.

UNITS PER SERVE • MEAT & ALT 1 • GRAIN 1 • VEG 3 • DAIRY 1 • OIL 2

Thai tofu skewers
with pickled cucumber

SERVES **4**
PREPARATION **35 MINUTES**
COOKING **15 MINUTES**

If you don't have skewers, just cut the tofu into cubes and serve them on top of the noodles. For non-vegetarians, chicken and fish make a great alternative to the tofu.

olive oil cooking spray
1 tablespoon red curry paste
650 g firm tofu, cut into
   2 cm pieces
juice of 1 lemon
320 g (2 cups) soaked brown rice
   vermicelli noodles
3 baby cos lettuce, shredded
160 g (2 cups) bean sprouts

Pickled cucumber
3 tablespoons white
   wine vinegar
2 teaspoons caster sugar
2 Lebanese cucumbers,
   finely sliced
1 small red onion, finely chopped
2 tablespoons finely
   chopped coriander
2 tablespoons toasted
   flaked almonds

To make the pickled cucumber, combine all the ingredients in a bowl and season to taste with freshly ground black pepper. Set aside until ready to serve.

Preheat the oven grill to high. Line a baking tray with foil and lightly spray the foil with oil.

Place the curry paste, tofu and lemon juice in a bowl and turn to coat well. Season with freshly ground black pepper.

Evenly thread the tofu onto metal skewers and lightly spray all over with oil. Cook under the grill for 10–12 minutes, turning occasionally, until heated through and golden crisp. If not using the skewers, place the cubes of tofu on the tray and, once each side is grilled, turn with tongs.

Divide the noodles, lettuce and bean sprouts among plates and top with the skewers. Spoon over the pickled cucumber, drizzle pickling vinegar over the noodles and salad, and serve.

UNITS PER SERVE • MEAT & ALT 1 • GRAIN 1 • VEGETABLES 3 • OIL 2

Weekend platters

MELON AND FETA SALAD

SPICED CARROT DIP

GRAZING PLATE

BABA GANOUSH
LAYERED DIP

MARINATED
BOCCONCINI AND
STRAWBERRY BITES

Weekend platters

Mealtimes over the weekend can often merge and meander. With this in mind, we've brought a range of recipes together that can be enjoyed whenever the occasion arises!

Spiced carrot dip

SERVES **4**
PREPARATION **25 MINUTES**
COOKING **10 MINUTES**

1 tablespoon olive oil
1 tablespoon Indian spice
    booster (see page 121)
3 medium carrots, chopped
120 g soft dried
    apricots, chopped
200 g reduced-fat cream cheese
1½ tablespoons toasted pumpkin
    seeds (pepitas)
crudités (cucumber, celery, sliced
    yellow squash, radish), to serve

Heat the oil in a saucepan over medium heat, add the spice booster and carrot and cook, stirring occasionally, for 5 minutes. Add the apricot and 125 ml (½ cup) water and simmer, stirring occasionally, for 5 minutes or until the carrot is soft and the water has evaporated. Cool slightly, transfer to a food processor, add the cream cheese and blend until smooth.

Scoop into a bowl and sprinkle with the pumpkin seeds. Serve with crudités.

Melon and feta salad

Re-imagine the classic feta-watermelon salad with this mixed melon version. The kids will love it too – cut back on herbs, if preferred, or omit the feta.

SERVES **4**
PREPARATION **15 MINUTES**

320 g (2 cups) sliced
    seedless watermelon
160 g (1 cup) sliced
    honeydew melon
160 g (1 cup) sliced rockmelon
160 g Greek feta, crumbled
finely grated zest and juice of
    1 large lemon
1 tablespoon extra virgin olive oil
½ cup small mint leaves
⅓ cup oregano leaves
1 cup flat-leaf parsley leaves
3 teaspoons mixed seeds
    (linseeds, sunflower seeds,
    pumpkin seeds/pepitas)

Place all the ingredients in a bowl and gently toss. Season with freshly ground black pepper and serve.

Grazing plate

A platter can go well beyond big slabs of cheese and crackers. Add a wow factor with these nutrient-dense accompaniments. The quantities in this recipe provide a guide but the amounts can be adjusted depending on numbers.

SERVES **4**
PREPARATION **5 MINUTES**

1 apple, thinly sliced
1 pear, thinly sliced
150 g strawberries
    and/or blueberries
2 tablespoons unsalted nuts
160 g portion of 1 cheese, or
    80 g portions of 2 cheeses
60 g muscatels
small bowls filled with your
    choice of: dill pickles,
    chargrilled capsicum in brine,
    artichokes in brine, marinated
    mushrooms, raw vegetable
    crudités, olives
12 rye crispbreads

Baba ganoush layered dip

This flavour-packed dip deserves to be the centre of attention as part of a Middle Eastern mezze platter, or it can be enjoyed on its own. Accompaniments could include raw vegetable crudités, toasted pita bread, olives, dolmades and hummus.

SERVES **4**
PREPARATION **20 MINUTES**
COOKING **15 MINUTES**

2 medium eggplants, thickly sliced
120 g soft dried figs
2 tablespoons tahini
2 teaspoons smoked paprika
finely grated zest and juice of 1 large lemon
2 large vine-ripened tomatoes, finely chopped
2 spring onions, thinly sliced
160 g Danish feta, crumbled
½ cup small mixed herb leaves (coriander, flat-leaf parsley, mint)
3 baby cos lettuces, leaves separated

Preheat a large chargrill pan over high heat. Working in two batches, chargrill the eggplant slices for 5–7 minutes each or until cooked and golden. Transfer to a food processor. Add the figs, tahini, paprika, lemon zest and juice to the food processor and blitz until almost smooth, adding a little water if needed to loosen slightly. Season with freshly ground black pepper.

Spread the baba ganoush mixture over the base of a large serving plate.

Combine the tomato and onion, then sprinkle evenly over the baba ganoush. Scatter with the feta, then the herbs and serve. Use the baby cos leaves to scoop up the dip.

Marinated bocconcini and strawberry bites

SERVES **4**
PREPARATION **25 MINUTES, PLUS CHILLING TIME**

1 tablespoon extra virgin olive oil
3 teaspoons Italian spice booster (see page 121)
2 tablespoons balsamic vinegar
600 g large strawberries, hulled and halved
200 g baby bocconcini
basil leaves, for wrapping
1½ tablespoons toasted flaked almonds

Place the oil, spice booster, vinegar, strawberries and bocconcini in a bowl and season with freshly ground black pepper. Stir to combine, then marinate in the fridge for 30 minutes to 1 hour (no longer or they will turn to mush).

Wrap each bocconcini in a basil leaf, then thread onto cocktail toothpicks with the strawberries. Arrange on a serving plate, sprinkle with the almonds and serve.

weekend dinner

Roast crumbed chicken with mushroom sauce

SERVES **4**
PREPARATION **30 MINUTES**
COOKING **30 MINUTES**

This is comfort food at its healthiest best! Enjoy the crispy crumb on the chicken and the smooth flavours of the mushroom sauce. Make this recipe go further by adding more vegetables, such as zucchini, broccoli and onion, to the roasting tin.

---

2 spring onions, thinly sliced

2 x 40 g slices wholemeal sourdough, processed to coarse crumbs

2 cloves garlic, thinly sliced

2 tablespoons toasted walnuts, finely chopped

finely grated zest and juice of 1 lemon

600 g chicken tenderloins

900 g tomatoes, cut into wedges, or cherry tomatoes

olive oil cooking spray

480 g (3 cups) cooked brown rice (see page 99)

mixed salad leaves and lemon wedges, to serve

Mushroom sauce

2 tablespoons light margarine

2 cloves garlic, crushed

1 onion, finely chopped

500 g button mushrooms, sliced

1 cup (250 ml) salt-reduced chicken stock

1 tablespoon Dijon mustard

2 tablespoons finely chopped flat-leaf parsley

Preheat the oven to 220°C (200°C fan-forced).

Combine the spring onion, breadcrumbs, garlic, walnuts, lemon zest and juice in a bowl. Press lightly and evenly onto the chicken strips and season with freshly ground black pepper. Spread the tomatoes over the base of a roasting tin and top with the chicken strips. Lightly spray all over with oil and roast for 25–30 minutes or until cooked and golden.

Meanwhile, to make the mushroom sauce, melt the margarine in a frying pan over medium–high heat. Add the garlic, onion and mushroom and cook, stirring, for 3 minutes or until golden and starting to soften. Reduce the heat to medium–low, pour in the stock and simmer gently for 12–15 minutes or until reduced by three-quarters. Remove the pan from the heat, stir through the mustard and parsley, and season with freshly ground black pepper.

Divide the rice, chicken and tomatoes among plates and spoon the mushroom sauce alongside. Serve with mixed salad leaves and lemon wedges.

UNITS PER SERVE • MEAT & ALT 1.5 • GRAIN 2 • VEGETABLES 3 • OIL 2

Chicken and pumpkin panang curry

SERVES **4**
PREPARATION **25 MINUTES**
COOKING **15 MINUTES**

This is a wonderful warming winter recipe for the whole family. If you like a bit of spice you can add a little chilli or extra curry paste. For a vegetarian option, replace chicken with cooked chickpeas, or other legume of your choice.

1 tablespoon panang curry paste
600 g diced chicken breast fillet
1 large red onion, cut
    into wedges
900 g peeled pumpkin, cut into
    1–2 cm cubes
450 g chat potatoes, cut
    into quarters
1.5 litres salt-reduced
    chicken stock
300 g sugar snap peas, trimmed
1 large red capsicum, seeded
    and chopped
480 g (3 cups) soaked brown rice
    vermicelli noodles
2 tablespoons toasted cashews,
    finely chopped

Heat a large, deep non-stick frying pan over medium heat. Add the curry paste, chicken and onion and cook, stirring, for 2 minutes. Add the pumpkin, potato and stock. Bring to a simmer, stirring, then reduce the heat to medium–low and simmer, stirring occasionally, for 10 minutes or until the vegetables are almost cooked.

Add the sugar snaps and capsicum and cook, stirring occasionally, for 3 minutes or until just tender.

Divide the noodles among bowls and spoon the panang curry over the top. Sprinkle with cashews and serve.

UNITS PER SERVE • MEAT & ALT 1.5 • GRAIN 2 • VEGETABLES 3 • OIL 2

Moroccan chicken casserole

SERVES **4**
PREPARATION **30 MINUTES**
COOKING **35 MINUTES**

Moroccan cuisine is often enhanced with dried fruit, such as apricots, dates, figs or raisins. Try finely chopping them and adding them to the couscous in this dish. If you don't have any couscous, use brown rice, quinoa or freekeh.

1 tablespoon olive oil

2 tablespoons Moroccan seasoning

2 red onion, cut into thick wedges

2 large sticks celery, cut into 3 cm lengths

2 large carrots, cut into 3 cm pieces

600 g orange sweet potato, cut into 3 cm pieces

600 g chicken tenderloins, halved widthways

2 litres salt-reduced chicken stock, heated

4 large kale leaves, white stalks removed, leaves finely shredded

200 g (1 cup) wholegrain couscous

2 tablespoons toasted unsalted pistachio kernels, finely chopped

1 cup small mixed herb leaves (coriander, flat-leaf parsley, mint)

lemon wedges, to serve

Heat the oil in a large, deep frying pan over medium heat. Add the seasoning, onion, celery and carrot and cook, stirring occasionally, for 5 minutes. Add the sweet potato, chicken and 1.5 litres of the stock. Bring to a simmer, stirring, then reduce the heat to medium–low and simmer gently, stirring occasionally, for 30 minutes or until cooked and the sauce has reduced by three-quarters.

Meanwhile, place the kale, couscous and remaining hot stock in a large bowl and stir well to combine. Cover and stand, untouched, for 10 minutes or until all the liquid has been absorbed, the kale has wilted and the couscous has expanded. Fluff up the grains with a fork and season with freshly ground black pepper.

Divide the kale couscous among serving plates and spoon over the casserole. Sprinkle with pistachios and herbs and serve with lemon wedges alongside.

UNITS PER SERVE • MEAT & ALT **1.5** • GRAIN **2** • VEGETABLES **3** • OIL **2**

Crispy salmon and slow-roasted vegetable linguini

SERVES **4**
PREPARATION **30 MINUTES**
COOKING **2 HOURS 10 MINUTES**

Finger eggplants add to the 'fancy factor' in this recipe, but two regular eggplants would work too. Feel free to try other types of fish, such as Australian mackerel, pink snapper or flathead.

---

4 roma tomatoes,
    halved lengthways
2 red onions, cut into wedges
8 finger eggplants,
    halved lengthways
2 tablespoons balsamic vinegar
2 teaspoons brown sugar
2 tablespoons rosemary leaves
olive oil cooking spray
640 g (4 cups) cooked linguine
4 x 150 g boneless salmon
    portions, skin on
2 tablespoons toasted slivered
    almonds, chopped
mixed micro herbs and lemon
    wedges, to serve

Preheat the oven to 170°C (150°C fan forced).

Combine the tomato, onion, eggplant, balsamic vinegar, sugar and rosemary in a large heavy-based baking dish. Season with freshly ground black pepper and spray lightly with oil. Slow-roast for 1½–2 hours or until very soft and golden.

Remove the vegetables from the oven. Add the cooked linguine and toss to combine and coat in the mixture. Cover, then set aside.

Preheat the oven grill to high. Line a baking tray with foil and spray with oil.

Place the salmon portions on the prepared tray, skin-side up, and pat the skins dry with paper towel. Cook, untouched, under the grill for 8–10 minutes or until the flesh is cooked to medium and the skin is crisp.

Divide the linguine mixture among serving plates and place the salmon on top, skin-side up. Sprinkle with almonds and micro herbs, and serve with lemon wedges alongside.

UNITS PER SERVE • MEAT & ALT 1.5 • GRAIN 2 • VEGETABLES 2+ • OIL 2

Seafood chowder

SERVES **4**
PREPARATION **35 MINUTES,
PLUS STANDING TIME**
COOKING **35 MINUTES**

Seafood marinara mixes can be bought from any fishmonger and most supermarket delicatessens. You could also use your own combination of fish, prawns, calamari and mussels.

---

1 head cauliflower, florets
    separated, stem chopped
2 bulbs fennel, trimmed
    and chopped
2 leeks, rinsed well and
    thinly sliced
800 g peeled potatoes, chopped
1 tablespoon sweet paprika
1.5 litres salt-reduced
    chicken stock
2 tablespoons olive oil
600 g fresh raw seafood
    marinara mix
2 cloves garlic, crushed
2 tablespoons chopped dill

Place the cauliflower, fennel, leek, potato, paprika and stock in a large saucepan over medium heat and cook, stirring, until the mixture comes to a simmer. Simmer, partially covered and stirring occasionally, for 20–25 minutes or until the vegetables are very tender. Remove the pan from the heat and stand for 10 minutes, then use a stick blender to blend the soup until completely smooth. Season with freshly ground black pepper. Cover to keep warm and set aside.

Heat the oil in a large, non-stick frying pan over high heat. Working in three batches, fry the seafood for 2 minutes each or until just cooked and light golden, adding the garlic in the last batch. Transfer to a bowl.

Divide the chowder among bowls and top with the seafood. Sprinkle with dill and serve.

UNITS PER SERVE • MEAT & ALT 1.5 • GRAIN 2 • VEGETABLES 3+ • OIL 2

White fish with salsa verde and baby potatoes

SERVES 4
PREPARATION 20 MINUTES
COOKING 15 MINUTES

The herbs in the salsa verde can be varied to suit your taste. Similarly, gherkins can be replaced with capers, and you can add extra olive oil for a runnier sauce. If you don't have a food processor, just chop up the herbs, garlic and gherkins by hand or grind up with a mortar and pestle. Any firm-fleshed white fish fillets work well here – try ling, blue-eye trevalla, coral trout, mahi mahi, snapper or cod.

600 g baby potatoes
olive oil cooking spray
4 x 150 g boneless firm white fish
   fillets, skin on

Salsa verde
1 cup flat-leaf parsley leaves
1 cup basil leaves
½ cup mint leaves
2 cloves garlic, roughly chopped
finely grated zest and juice of
   1 lemon
1 tablespoon chopped gherkins
1 tablespoon Dijon mustard
2 teaspoons red wine vinegar
1 tablespoon olive oil

Salad
4 cups mixed lettuce leaves
2 vine-ripened tomatoes, cut into
   wedges
300 g sugar snap peas, trimmed
2 red capsicums, seeded and
   thinly sliced

Boil the baby potatoes in a large saucepan of water over high heat for 8–10 minutes or until tender.

Meanwhile, to make the salsa verde, place all the ingredients in a food processor and process until smooth. Season with freshly ground black pepper.

Lightly spray a large non-stick frying pan with oil and heat over medium heat. Add the fish, skin-side down, and cook for 3–4 minutes, then turn over and cook for another 1–2 minutes.

Divide the salad ingredients and potatoes among serving plates and top with the fish fillets. Spoon over the salsa verde and serve.

UNITS PER SERVE • MEAT & ALT 1.5 • GRAIN 2 • VEGETABLES 3 • OIL 1

ALL-PURPOSE CHICKEN

MEXICAN CHICKEN AND BEAN

ASIAN PORK

Slow-cook dinners

INDIAN BEEF
AND CHICKPEA

ITALIAN LAMB

Slow-cook dinners

The flavours in these dinners can be tailored to your individual taste with additions such as chilli, herbs, sumac, capers, anchovies, salsa verde or mustard. A range of vegetables can be included – use whatever is left in the fridge! These meals have been designed to be prepared ahead on weekends in large batches. Let the flavours develop over a few days, then enjoy a meal ready to heat and serve. If you don't have a slow cooker, place the ingredients (other than the grain and 'toppers') in a heavy, lidded ovenproof stockpot and cook in a preheated 160°C (140°C fan-forced) oven for 4 hours.

Heat the oil in a large, deep non-stick frying pan over high heat. Add the spice booster and meat or alternative protein and cook, tossing, until just seared. Transfer the mixture to a slow cooker.

Add the vegetables and stock. Cover and cook on high for 6 hours, stirring occasionally.

Prepare the grain (see page 96) and divide among serving bowls, then spoon on the slow-cooker portion. Serve sprinkled with the 'toppers'.

EACH DINNER SERVES 4

To make ahead and freeze

Allow the slow-cooker meal to cool slightly. Divide the grain among individual freezer-safe containers, then spoon on the slow-cooker portion. Cover and freeze. Thaw in the fridge overnight and gently reheat on the stovetop or in the microwave on medium. Make sure your meal is piping hot throughout before eating.

UNITS PER SERVE • MEAT & ALT 1.5 • GRAIN 2 • VEGETABLES 3 • OIL 2

All-purpose chicken

2 tablespoons olive oil
2 tablespoons All-purpose spice
    booster (see page 122)
600 g diced chicken breast
2 carrots, chopped
3 sticks celery, sliced
2 green capsicums, seeded,
    cut into 3 cm pieces
1 cup (250 ml) salt-reduced
    chicken stock
640 g (4 cups) cooked brown rice
    (see page 99)

Topper
chopped flat-leaf parsley
1 bunch English spinach, leaves
    picked and wilted

Mexican chicken
and bean

2 tablespoons olive oil
2 tablespoons Mexican spice
    booster (see page 122)
400 g diced chicken breast
400 g tin red kidney beans,
    drained and rinsed
2 red onions, chopped
3 carrots, chopped
3 zucchini, chopped
1 cup (250 ml) salt-reduced
    chicken stock
640 g (4 cups) cooked
    wholegrain penne

Topper
coriander leaves
3 cups mixed salad greens
lime wedges

Indian beef
and chickpea

2 tablespoons olive oil
2 tablespoons Indian spice
    booster (see page 121)
400 g diced beef
400 g tin chickpeas, drained
    and rinsed
2 red onions, chopped
3 sticks celery, chopped
2 carrots, chopped
1 cup (250 ml) salt-reduced
    beef stock
720 g (4 cups) cooked quinoa
    (see page 99)

Topper
coriander and mint leaves
3 cups baby spinach leaves

Asian pork

2 tablespoons olive oil
2 tablespoons Asian spice
    booster (see page 122)
600 g diced pork
1 red onion, chopped
3 sticks celery, chopped
2 red capsicums, seeded,
    cut into 3 cm pieces
1 cup (250 ml) salt-reduced
    chicken stock
720 g (4 cups) cooked buckwheat
    (see page 96)

Topper
coriander leaves
3 pieces baby bok choy, halved
    and steamed

Italian lamb

2 tablespoons olive oil
2 tablespoons Italian spice
    booster (see page 121)
600 g diced lamb
2 leeks, chopped
4 carrots, chopped
1 bulb fennel, chopped
1 cup (250 ml) salt-reduced
    beef stock
720 g (4 cups) cooked pearl
    barley (see page 99)

Topper
basil leaves
1 bunch silverbeet, white cores
    removed, wilted

FOR A VEGETARIAN OPTION, REPLACE LAMB WITH A COMBINATION OF CANNELLINI BEANS AND LIMA BEANS, AND REDUCE THE COOKING TIME TO 2 HOURS.

Slow-cooked pulled beef

SERVES **4**
PREPARATION **25 MINUTES**
COOKING **6 HOURS**

This dish is ideal to share with friends. Bulk up the pulled beef by doubling the quantities or adding a couple of tins of drained black beans. An alternative way to serve this is to provide a pile of soft tacos, grated cheese, lettuce and salsa for your guests to make their own pulled-beef burritos.

600 g diced beef
2 tablespoons Mexican spice
  booster (see page 122)
400 g tin crushed tomatoes
1 red onion, thickly sliced
2 zucchini, cut into
  1 cm-thick matchsticks
4 red capsicums, seeded and
  thickly sliced
640 g (4 cups) cooked brown
  basmati rice (see page 99)
160 g sliced avocado
1 cup rocket leaves
1 cup small coriander sprigs
lime wedges, to serve

Set a slow cooker to high and cover.

Add the beef, spice booster, tomatoes, onion and 125 ml (½ cup) water to the slow cooker and stir until well combined. Cook on high, untouched, for 4 hours.

Place the zucchini on top of the beef mixture, followed by the red capsicum. Cook on high for a further 2 hours.

Divide the rice among bowls, then top with the capsicum and zucchini. Using two forks, shred the beef mixture in the slow cooker, then spoon over the vegetables in the bowls. Top with the avocado, rocket and coriander sprigs and serve with lime wedges alongside.

UNITS PER SERVE • MEAT & ALT 1.5 • GRAIN 2 • VEGETABLES 3 • OIL 2

Beef, bean and barley casserole

SERVES 4
PREPARATION **25 MINUTES,
PLUS STANDING TIME**
COOKING **1 HOUR 10 MINUTES**

This comforting casserole with a fresh zingy topping is sure to be a family favourite. If you have bigger appetites to cater for, simply increase the quantity of beans and barley.

2 tablespoons olive oil
400 g diced beef
1 onion, chopped
600 g small button mushrooms
200 g (1 cup) pearl barley
2 litres salt-reduced beef stock
400 g tin cannellini beans,
 drained and rinsed
4 cups mixed salad greens
2 Lebanese cucumbers, sliced

Zesty sprinkle
3 tablespoons finely chopped
 flat-leaf parsley
1 small clove garlic,
 finely chopped
3 teaspoons finely grated
 lemon zest
1 long red chilli, seeded and
 finely chopped (optional)

To make the zesty sprinkle, combine all the ingredients in a bowl. Cover and chill until ready to serve.

Heat the oil in a large saucepan over high heat, add the beef and cook, stirring, for 2–3 minutes or until browned. Reduce the heat to medium. Add the onion and mushrooms and cook, stirring occasionally, for 3 minutes or until starting to soften. Add the barley and stock and bring to a simmer. Reduce the heat to medium–low and simmer gently, stirring occasionally, for 1 hour or until the beef is very tender and the sauce has reduced by three-quarters. Stir in the beans, then remove the pan from the heat. Cover and leave to stand for 10 minutes.

Divide the casserole among bowls and top with the zesty sprinkle. Serve with salad greens and cucumber alongside.

UNITS PER SERVE • **MEAT & ALT 1.5** • **GRAIN 2** • **VEGETABLES 3** • **OIL 2**

Lamb ragu with olives and polenta

SERVES **4**
PREPARATION **30 MINUTES**
COOKING **4 HOURS 10 MINUTES**

Polenta is a staple in many parts of Italy and makes a wonderful accompaniment to this ragu. The ragu can be stored in the fridge for up to 3 days or frozen. Thaw the frozen mixture in the fridge overnight and reheat in a large saucepan over medium heat, ensuring it is heated throughout before eating.

600 g diced lamb
1 head garlic, outer leaves
    removed, halved horizontally
4 large zucchini, thickly sliced
2 large red capsicums, seeded
    and thickly sliced
2 large green capsicums, seeded
    and thickly sliced
2 red onions, cut into
    thick wedges
2 lemons, cut into wedges
1 small bunch oregano
3 tablespoons pitted kalamata
    olives, halved
1 litre salt-reduced chicken stock
170 g (1 cup) instant polenta
1 tablespoon olive oil
rocket or other leafy greens,
    to serve

Preheat the oven to 160°C (140°C fan-forced).

Combine the lamb, garlic, zucchini, capsicum, onion, lemon, oregano, olives and 500 ml (2 cups) of the stock in a large, heavy-based roasting tin. Cover with a double layer of foil and slow-roast for 4 hours or until very tender. Remove and set aside to rest.

Heat the remaining stock in a saucepan over medium heat. Slowly whisk the polenta into the hot stock, making sure no lumps form. Cook, whisking constantly, for 5–7 minutes or until the polenta is very thick and the grains are tender. Remove the pan from the heat and whisk in the olive oil until melted and well combined. Season with freshly ground black pepper.

Divide the polenta among plates and spoon the lamb ragu over the top. Serve with rocket or other leafy greens.

UNITS PER SERVE • **MEAT & ALT** 1.5 • **GRAIN** 2 • **VEGETABLES** 3 • **OIL** 2

Eggplant with garlic crumbs and butter bean sweet potato mash

SERVES **4**
PREPARATION **30 MINUTES**
COOKING **30 MINUTES**

If you are short of time, you can buy chargrilled eggplant slices from the deli counter at the supermarket. Fancy a change from lettuce? Try watercress here, instead – the deep green leaves will bring a welcome peppery flavour to the dish.

3 medium eggplants, sliced
 into 1 cm thick rounds
2 tablespoons olive oil
2 cloves garlic, crushed
2 tablespoons finely
 chopped rosemary
4 x 40 g slices multigrain bread,
 processed to crumbs
300 g Quorn™ mince
 or other plant-based mince
2 spring onions, sliced
lemon wedges, to serve

Butter bean sweet potato mash
600 g peeled and chopped
 orange sweet potato
2 x 400 g tins butter beans,
 drained and rinsed
2 tablespoons light margarine
1 clove garlic, crushed

Salad
3 cups mixed lettuce leaves
2 cucumbers, sliced
1 green capsicum, seeded
 and sliced
2 spring onions, sliced
1 stick celery, thinly sliced

To make the mash, boil the sweet potato in a large saucepan of water over high heat for 12–15 minutes or until tender. Drain well, then return to the pan with all the remaining ingredients. Reduce the heat to medium–low and cook, stirring, for 3–4 minutes or until heated through. Remove from the heat and roughly mash together. Cover to keep warm and set aside.

Meanwhile, heat half the oil in a large, deep non-stick frying pan over medium–high heat. Working in batches, cook the eggplant for 5 minutes or until cooked and golden. Transfer to a plate and cover.

Reheat the frying pan over medium–high heat and add half the remaining oil, half the garlic, half the rosemary and all the breadcrumbs. Cook, stirring constantly, for 1–2 minutes or until the crumbs are lightly golden. Transfer to a bowl.

Return the pan to the heat and add the Quorn and the remaining oil, garlic and rosemary. Cook, stirring and breaking up any large pieces of Quorn with a spoon, for 5 minutes or until heated through and golden crisp. Add to the breadcrumb mixture and stir well to combine. Season with freshly ground black pepper.

Toss together all the salad ingredients. Layer the eggplant slices and garlic crumb mixture evenly onto plates and dollop the butter bean sweet potato mash alongside. Serve with the salad, scattered with spring onion and with the lemon wedges alongside.

UNITS PER SERVE • **MEAT & ALT** 1.5 • **GRAIN** 2 • **VEGETABLES** 3 • **OIL** 2

Mushroom and leek shepherds pie

SERVES **4**
PREPARATION **30 MINUTES**
COOKING **40 MINUTES**

The spinach can be replaced with Swiss chard, kale or collard greens, though these will require a little extra cooking. Use lean beef mince for a non-vegetarian option.

---

600 g Quorn™ 'mince'
  or other plant-based mince
2 tablespoons light margarine
2 leeks, white part only,
  thinly sliced
300 g button mushrooms, halved
2 tablespoons Italian spice
  booster (see page 121)
2 tablespoons salt-reduced
  soy sauce
2 cups (500 ml) salt-reduced
  vegetable stock
4 cups baby spinach leaves
olive oil cooking spray

Potato topping
1.2 kg potatoes, peeled and
  cut into 2 cm chunks
2 tablespoons light margarine
3 tablespoons finely
  chopped mixed herbs
  (thyme, flat-leaf parsley)

Heat a large, deep non-stick frying pan over high heat, add the 'mince' and cook, stirring constantly and breaking up any large pieces with a spoon, for 5 minutes or until cooked through and golden. Reduce the heat to medium. Add the margarine, leek, mushroom and spice booster and cook, stirring occasionally, for 10 minutes or until very soft. Add the soy sauce and stock and simmer, stirring occasionally, for 10–12 minutes or until the liquid has reduced by three-quarters. Add 2 cups of baby spinach and cook, stirring, for 2–3 minutes or until wilted.

Meanwhile, to make the topping, cook the potatoes in a large saucepan of boiling water over high heat for 12–15 minutes or until tender. Drain well, then return to the pan. Add the margarine and fresh herbs and mash together until smooth. Season with freshly ground black pepper. Cover to keep warm and set aside.

Position the shelf lower in the oven. Preheat the oven grill to medium–high.

Spoon the 'mince' mixture into a deep flameproof 1.5 litre baking dish and spread evenly with the potato topping, using a fork to create a pattern all over the surface. Spray lightly with oil and cook under the grill for 6–8 minutes or until the top is golden and crispy. Take the dish straight to the table and serve with the remaining baby spinach leaves.

UNITS PER SERVE • MEAT & ALT **1.5** • GRAIN **2** • VEGETABLES **3** • OIL **2**

weekend dessert

Custard brulée with choc pastries

WEEKEND DESSERT

SERVES **4**
PREPARATION **30 MINUTES,
PLUS COOLING TIME**
COOKING **15 MINUTES**

No blowtorch? No problem. Pop your ramekins under your oven grill for about 5 minutes until the sugar turns a deep golden. The custard can be prepared the day before and refrigerated in an airtight container; when you're ready to serve, allow the custard to come to room temperature before bruléeing.

---

8 sheets filo pastry
olive oil cooking spray
80 g dark chocolate,
  finely grated
400 ml custard
100 g reduced-fat cream cheese,
  at room temperature
2 tablespoons caster sugar

Preheat the oven to 200°C (180°C fan-forced). Line 2 large baking trays with baking paper.

Lay out the filo sheets on a work surface and lightly spray the tops with oil. Sprinkle the chocolate evenly over seven of the sheets, then stack them directly on top of each other. Finish with the remaining piece of filo and press down lightly. Cut the stack into 12 even pieces, then transfer to the prepared trays.

Place both trays in the oven and bake for 10–12 minutes, turning the trays around on the shelves halfway through, until the pastries are cooked and golden. Cool on the trays, then transfer the pastries to serving plates.

Using a hand-held electric mixer, beat the custard and cream cheese until smooth. Divide among four 180 ml flameproof ramekins, then level the surface and sprinkle the tops evenly with sugar. Use a blowtorch to caramelise the sugar until it melts and turns deep golden. Allow the caramelised sugar to set, then serve with the chocolate pastries alongside.

UNITS PER SERVE • DAIRY 1 • INDULGENCES 2

THE CUSTARD BRULÉES ARE SO SIMPLE TO PREPARE. YOU COULD LEAVE OUT THE PASTRIES AND MAKE THEM IN MINUTES.

Sangria pear jellies

WEEKEND
DESSERT

SERVES **4**
PREPARATION **15 MINUTES, PLUS
STANDING AND CHILLING TIME**
COOKING **15 MINUTES**

Although the alcohol is cooked out of these jellies, they are likely to appeal more to adults and would make a perfect dinner party dessert. Use grape juice instead of wine to make them more child-friendly. These jellies can be made up to a day in advance; just cover and keep chilled until you are ready to serve.

---

600 ml red wine (or grape juice)
2 cinnamon sticks, broken
3 star anise
4 cloves
4 strips orange rind
4 strips lemon rind
4 firm ripe pears, peeled, cored
   and chopped
1 tablespoon powdered gelatine

Place the wine (or grape juice), spices, citrus rind and 1 cup (250 ml) water in a large saucepan over medium–low heat and cook gently for 15 minutes. Remove from the heat and discard the spices and rind. Add the pear to the spiced wine and leave, covered, for 15 minutes.

Whisk the gelatine into the wine and pear mixture, then ladle evenly into 4 serving glasses. Cool to room temperature, then transfer to the fridge for 2 hours or until set. Serve.

UNITS PER SERVE • FRUIT 1 • INDULGENCES 2

Strawberry crumble

WEEKEND
DESSERT

SERVES 4
PREPARATION 15 MINUTES
COOKING 15 MINUTES

This is a great chance for the kids to help out in the kitchen. The whole family will ask for seconds of this simple and tasty treat. If fresh strawberries are not in season, frozen strawberries work well too.

---

600 g strawberries, hulled
   and halved
3 teaspoons balsamic vinegar
2 teaspoons pure vanilla extract
75 g (½ cup) plain flour
45 g (½ cup) rolled oats
½ teaspoon mixed spice
1 tablespoon brown sugar
2 tablespoons light margarine
½ teaspoon icing sugar

Preheat the oven to 200°C (180°C fan-forced).

Place the strawberries in a 20 cm round pie plate. Drizzle with the balsamic and vanilla and toss to coat well. Set aside.

Combine the flour, oats, mixed spice and brown sugar in a bowl. Add the margarine and gently rub together until rough crumbs form.

Sprinkle the crumble over the strawberry mixture and bake for 12–15 minutes or until the top is golden and the fruit is bubbling. Dust with icing sugar and serve.

UNITS PER SERVE • FRUIT 1 • INDULGENCES 2

Coffee creams with choc-drizzled sponge fingers

SERVES **4**
PREPARATION **20 MINUTES,
PLUS CHILLING TIME**

Ramp up the 'fancy factor' by using a shot of espresso in place of the instant coffee and grating some extra dark chocolate over the coffee cream prior to serving.

50 g reduced-fat cream cheese

150 g fresh ricotta

2 teaspoons instant coffee dissolved in 3 teaspoons boiling water, or 1 shot of espresso

1 teaspoon pure vanilla extract

2 teaspoons pure maple syrup

80 g dark chocolate

8 savoiardi (sponge finger biscuits)

Using an electric hand-held mixer, blend the cream cheese, ricotta, coffee mixture, vanilla and maple syrup until very smooth. Spoon into four small ramekins or glasses and chill for at least 30 minutes.

Break the chocolate into a microwave-safe bowl and melt on medium in 30-second bursts until smooth and melted, stirring between bursts. Alternatively, melt the chocolate in a heatproof bowl set over a small saucepan of very gently simmering water, stirring constantly.

Place the savoiardi on a baking tray lined with baking paper and drizzle the tops with the melted chocolate. Chill for about 20 minutes until set.

Serve the chilled coffee creams with the choc-drizzled sponge fingers for dipping.

UNITS PER SERVE • DAIRY 1 • INDULGENCES 2

More information

Key references

Institute of Medicine (US) and National Research Council (US) Committee to Reexamine IOM Pregnancy Weight Guidelines. 2009. *Weight Gain During Pregnancy: Reexamining the Guidelines.* National Academies Press (US); 2009.

National Health and Medical Research Council. 2013. *Australian Dietary Guidelines.* Canberra: National Health and Medical Research Council.

National Health and Medical Research Council. 2006. *Nutrient Reference Values for Australia and New Zealand.* Canberra: National Health and Medical Research Council.

Websites that provide useful, credible information.

Fertility
www.yourfertility.org.au

Healthy eating
Australian Dietary Guidelines:
www.eatforhealth.gov.au

Search for an Accredited Practising Dietitian (APD): dietitiansaustralia.org.au/find-an-apd

CSIRO Weight Management Programs and Dietary Tools:
www.csiro.au/en/Research/Health/CSIRO-diets
Food Safety:
www.foodstandards.gov.au/foodsafety

Healthy habits
Alcohol:
www.nhmrc.gov.au/health-advice/alcohol
Smoking: www.icanquit.com.au
Creating healthy habits:
www.healthdirect.gov.au/creating-healthy-habits

Physical activity
www.health.gov.au/health-topics/exercise-and-physical-activity

Pregnancy and breastfeeding
www.healthdirect.gov.au/pregnancy

Puberty
raisingchildren.net.au/teens/development

Women's Health
Women's health advice across the lifespan:
www.jeanhailes.org.au

The Heart Foundation:
www.heartfoundation.org.au

Cancer Council: www.cancer.org.au

Diabetes Australia:
www.diabetesaustralia.com.au

Osteoporosis Australia: www.osteoporosis.org.au
Brain Health: www.dementia.org.au

Recipe conversion chart

Measuring cups and spoons may vary slightly from one country to another, but the difference is generally not enough to affect a recipe. All cup and spoon measures are level.

One Australian metric measuring cup holds 250 ml (8 fl oz), one Australian tablespoon holds 20 ml (4 teaspoons) and one Australian metric teaspoon holds 5 ml. North America, New Zealand and the UK use a 15 ml (3-teaspoon) tablespoon.

LENGTH

METRIC	IMPERIAL
3 mm	⅛ inch
6 mm	¼ inch
1 cm	½ inch
2.5 cm	1 inch
5 cm	2 inches
18 cm	7 inches
20 cm	8 inches
23 cm	9 inches
25 cm	10 inches
30 cm	12 inches

LIQUID MEASURES

ONE AMERICAN PINT	ONE IMPERIAL PINT
500 ml (16 fl oz)	600 ml (20 fl oz)

CUP	METRIC	IMPERIAL
⅛ cup	30 ml	1 fl oz
¼ cup	60 ml	2 fl oz
⅓ cup	80 ml	2½ fl oz
½ cup	125 ml	4 fl oz
⅔ cup	160 ml	5 fl oz
¾ cup	180 ml	6 fl oz
1 cup	250 ml	8 fl oz
2 cups	500 ml	16 fl oz
2¼ cups	560 ml	20 fl oz
4 cups	1 litre	32 fl oz

DRY MEASURES

The most accurate way to measure dry ingredients is to weigh them. However, if using a cup, add the ingredient loosely to the cup and level with a knife; don't compact the ingredient unless the recipe requests 'firmly packed'.

METRIC	IMPERIAL
15 g	½ oz
30 g	1 oz
60 g	2 oz
125 g	4 oz (¼ lb)
185 g	6 oz
250 g	8 oz (½ lb)
375 g	12 oz (¾ lb)
500 g	16 oz (1 lb)
1 kg	32 oz (2 lb)

OVEN TEMPERATURES

CELSIUS	FAHRENHEIT	CELSIUS	GAS MARK
100°C	200°F	110°C	¼
120°C	250°F	130°C	½
150°C	300°F	140°C	1
160°C	325°F	150°C	2
180°C	350°F	170°C	3
200°C	400°F	180°C	4
220°C	425°F	190°C	5
		200°C	6
		220°C	7
		230°C	8
		240°C	9
		250°C	10

Acknowledgements

We sincerely thank the following eminent scientists who reviewed the book to ensure its accuracy and correct translation of complex science into actions for everyday life:

Prof Sarah Robertson, Director, Robinson Research Institute, University of Adelaide;

Dr Ivanka Prichard, Co-Deputy Director, SHAPE Research Centre, Flinders University;

Dr Melinda Hutchesson, Senior Lecturer (Nutrition & Dietetics), The University of Newcastle;

Prof Tim Green, Principal Nutritionist, Women and Kids, South Australian Health & Medical Research Institute; Affiliate Professor, School of Medicine, The University of Adelaide;

Prof Danielle Mazza, Head, Department of General Practice, Monash University and Director, SPHERE NHMRC Centre of Research Excellence in Sexual and Reproductive Health for Women in Primary Care.

We also acknowledge the many research teams globally for their groundbreaking research. Their scientific discoveries, position and consensus statements and evidence-based practise guidelines underpin the core principles outlined in this book and are such a valuable complement to our own knowledge. Now more than ever the world needs a robust global scientific community that collaborates to provide innovative science based solutions that address our many health challenges.

At CSIRO, thanks to Dr Rob Grenfell, Bianca Frew, Therese Willis and the whole CSIRO Nutrition and Health team for such an extraordinary track record in cutting-edge nutrition and health research, backed up by translation into practical resources that support the health of Australians. None of which is possible without the contribution of our many and generous clinical trial volunteers – thank you!

Our appreciation and thanks for the hard-working team at Pan Macmillan who share our passion for communicating science, promoting health and talking to women's unique health needs and experiences. Special mention to Ingrid Ohlsson, Ariane Durkin, Naomi van Groll, Libby Turner and Madeleine Kane, for sharing our vision, impeccable editing, production and attention to detail. Thank you to Clare Keighery and Adrik Kemp for spreading the important messages of this book. Thanks to Tracey Pattison who enhances this book with her beautiful recipes that meet our criteria for maximum nutrition, ease and flavour! To Elisabeth Hartmann-Smith and Allison Croft, a heartfelt thanks for capturing us so naturally.

And finally, we acknowledge our readers. Our goal is to provide you with the knowledge and tools to nourish your body across every stage of womanhood, dispel the myths and do away with habits that don't serve us so well. Thank you for trusting CSIRO to translate the scientific evidence into sensible advice and delicious food.

Index

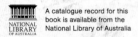

A catalogue record for this
book is available from the
National Library of Australia

Design by Madeleine Kane

Recipe design by Emily O'Neill

Cover design by Northwood Green

Recipe development by Tracey Pattison

Edited by Libby Turner and Rachel Carter

Index by Glenda Downing

Hair and makeup by Elisabeth
Hartmann-Smith

Prop and food styling by Emma Knowles

Food preparation by Kerrie Ray
with Dixie Elliot

Colour + reproduction by Splitting Image
Colour Studio

Printed in China by 1010 Printing
International Limited

We advise that the information contained in this book does not negate personal
responsibility on the part of the reader for their own health and safety. It is recommended
that individually tailored advice is sought from your healthcare or medical professional.
The publishers and their respective employees, agents and authors are not liable for
injuries or damage occasioned to any person as a result of reading or following the
information contained in this book.

10 9 8 7 6 5 4 3 2 1